Assessment

Wh t's in it fo schools?

Assessment is a prominent and sometimes controversial issue in education. This book looks at how and why assessment matters in the classroom, discussing key issues such as:

- Can assessment raise standards?
- Can current practice be improved?
- How does self-assessment help pupils learn?

Each chapter includes practical advice for teachers on how to move from assessment that merely measures and certifies to that which is an integral and planned element of the learning process. This book is for all those who want to develop their understanding and use of assessment, to improve teaching and learning in their schools.

Paul Weeden is a Lecturer in Geography Education at the University of Birmingham. **Jan Winter** is a Lecturer and **Patricia Broadfoot** is Professor of Education, both at the Graduate School of Education, University of Bristol.

What's in it for schools?
Edited by Kate Myers and John MacBeath

Inspection: What's in it for schools?
James Learmonth

Leadership: What's in it for schools?
Thomas J. Sergiovanni

Self-evaluation: What's in it for schools?
John MacBeath and Archie McGlynn

School Improvement: What's in it for schools?
Alma Harris

Assessment: What's in it for schools?
Paul Weeden, Jan Winter and Patricia Broadfoot

Assessment

What's in it for schools?

Paul Weeden
Jan Winter
Patricia Broadfoot

RoutledgeFalmer
Taylor & Francis Group

LONDON AND NEW YORK

First published 2002
by RoutledgeFalmer
2 Park Square, Milton Park, Abingdon, Oxon, OX14 4RN

Simultaneously published in the USA and Canada
by RoutledgeFalmer
270 Madison Ave, New York, NY 10016

Reprinted 2004, 2005

RoutledgeFalmer is an imprint of the Taylor & Francis Group

© 2002 Paul Weeden, Jan Winter and Patricia Broadfoot

Typeset in Baskerville by
Keystroke, Jacaranda Lodge, Wolverhampton
Printed and bound in Great Britain by
TJ International Ltd, Padstow, Cornwall

British Library Cataloguing in Publication Data
A catalogue record for this book is available from the British Library

Library of Congress Cataloging in Publication Data
A catalog record for this book has been requested.

ISBN 0–415–23591–X (hbk)
ISBN 0–415–23592–8 (pbk)

Contents

List of figures   vi
List of tables   vii
Acknowledgements   ix
Series Editors' preface   xi

1   Assessment: to measure or to learn?   1

2   Can assessment for learning raise standards?   18

3   Can current assessment practice be improved?   40

4   How does self-assessment help pupils learn?   72

5   How can marking and feedback help pupils learn?   95

6   Developing assessment for learning   122

7   Opening up the secret garden of assessment   150

References and further reading   156
Index   160

Figures

1.1 O-level and GCSE results (1980–2001)   3
1.2 Ascent of the A-level (1951–2000)   3
1.3 'Standards are rising' – are pupils becoming better
      learners?   4
1.4 'What do we have to do?' 'Don't worry – just do what
      I tell you.'   5
2.1 Teaching, learning and assessment   23
2.2 Clarity of goals leads to success   26
3.1 Are assessment methods successful?   43
3.2 Equality in gender performance?   60
3.3 Average exam scores by ethnic origin, gender and social
      class (England and Wales, 1985)   61
3.4 The long, hard road to disaffection   62
3.5 Appropriate learning style   67
4.1 Self-assessment   73
4.2 Learning briefing sheet   78
4.3 'We think we know where we went wrong!'   82
5.1 Effective questioning promotes learning   95
5.2 Maps of a school   99
5.3 Grades don't help pupils understand how to improve their
      performance   111
6.1 The well-planned lesson includes an opportunity for
      assessment   131
6.2 Effective questioning   138

Tables

2.1	Some definitions of assessment terminology	20
2.2	Definitions of validity, reliability and manageability	21
2.3	National qualifications framework	33
6.1	Key areas for developing assessment	124
6.2	Planning for assessment	133
6.3	A typology of assessment data-gathering methods	136

Acknowledgements

The authors would like to thank the following for permission to reproduce material:

Mike George for the cartoons

The *Times Educational Supplement* for Figures 1.1, 1.2 and 3.4

The Qualifications and Curriculum Authority for Table 2.3

The Geographical Association for Table 6.1

Table 6.3 reproduced from A. Pollard and P. Triggs, *Reflective Teaching in Secondary Education*, (1998) Continuum International Publishing Group, The Tower Building, 11 York Road, London, England.

Series Editors' preface

Kate Myers and John MacBeath

Series introduction

There is a concerted move to raise standards in the public education system. The aim is laudable. Few people would disagree with it. However, there is no clear agreement about what we mean by 'standards'. Do we mean attainment or achievement more broadly defined, for example, and how we are to raise whatever it is we agree needs raising?

At the same time, there appears to be an increasing trend towards approaching changes in education through a controlling, rational and technical framework. This framework tends to concentrate on educational content and delivery and ignores the human-resource perspective and the complexity of how human beings live, work and interact with one another. It overemphasizes linearity and pays insufficient attention to how people respond to change and either support or subvert it.

Recent government initiatives, including the National Curriculum, OFSTED school and LEA inspections, assessment procedures, league tables, target-setting, literacy and numeracy hours, and performance management have endorsed this framework. On occasions this has been less to do with the content of 'reforms' than the process of implementation – that is, doing it 'to' rather than 'with' the teaching profession. Teachers are frequently treated as the problem rather than part of the solution, with the consequence that many feel disillusioned, demoralised and disempowered. Critics of this *top-down* approach are often seen as lacking rigour, complacent about standards, and uninterested in raising achievement.

We wanted to edit this series because we believe that you can be passionate about public education, about raising achievement, about ensuring that all pupils are entitled to the best possible education that society is able to provide – whatever their race, sex or class. We also believe that achieving this is not a simple matter of common sense or of the appliance of science – it is more complex than that. Most of all, we see the teaching profession as an important part of the solution to finding ways through these complexities.

What's in it for schools? is a series that will make educational policy issues relevant to practitioners. Each book in the series focuses on a major educational issue and raises key questions, such as:

- Can inspection be beneficial to schools?
- How can assessment procedures help pupils learn?
- How can school self-evaluation improve teaching and learning?
- What impact does leadership in the school have in the classroom?
- How can school improvement become classroom improvement?

The books are grounded in sound theory, recent research evidence and best practice, and aim to:

- help you to make meaning personally and professionally from knowledge in a given field
- help you to seek out practical applications of an area of knowledge for classrooms and schools
- help those of you who want to research the field in greater depth, by providing key sources with accessible summaries and recommendations.

In addition, each chapter ends with a series of questions for reflection or further discussion, enabling schools to use the books as a resource for whole-school staff development.

We hope that the books in this series will show you that there are ways of raising achievement that can take account of how schools grow and develop and how teachers work and interact with one another. *What's in it for schools?* – a great deal, we think!

1 Assessment: to measure or to learn?

Standards are rising

Standards are going up in English schools. This at least is the judgement of the Office for Standards in Education (OFSTED), based on its inspections of schools during recent years. Both the 1999 Chief Inspector's report on English primary schools and the 1998 review of secondary education in England report rising levels of performance. For example, in primary schools:

> The quality of education in primary schools has improved . . . More children are achieving higher standards by the time they transfer to secondary school. At Key Stage 2 there has been a substantial increase in the proportion of pupils achieving Level 4 in English and mathematics. This proportion has risen by about 15 percentage points over the four years.
>
> (OFSTED, 1999: 9)

The 2001 National Curriculum assessment test results for Key Stages 1, 2 and 3 in England tell a similar story. In most areas progress has been made towards the targets set by the government for schools and Local Education Authorities (LEAs). So far, so good. There can be little doubt that the enormous effort that the government has put into raising standards in recent years has borne fruit.

Equally there is evidence from national examination results, GCSE and A level, that standards are going up at this level too. The government has met its target of 50 per cent of pupils achieving five or more

GCSE at grades A*–C or the GNVQ equivalent a year early (2001 rather than 2002). This has increased from 46.3 per cent in 1997 when the targets were announced.

Both Figure 1.1 and Figure 1.2 show how the grades achieved have risen over time. What does the rise in measured standards really mean? Are pupils better learners? Is teaching getting better? Are examinations getting easier? Despite the yearly complaints that GCSE and A-level examinations are getting easier, reports from the Qualifications and Curriculum Authority (QCA, 2001c) suggest there is no evidence to support this claim. So what is happening?

Are pupils becoming better learners?

Undoubtedly teachers are becoming better at preparing pupils to perform in these national tests. Does that mean that pupils are becoming better learners? Does the current emphasis on formal summative assessment in the shape of external tests and exams mean that pupils are becoming better equipped to be lifelong learners in the twenty-first century? Are pupils learning the right things in school? Are some pupils demotivated by assessment? Are we indeed paying a price for the growing emphasis on performance that is necessarily dominating teachers' and pupils' minds in today's schools? If so, what can teachers do about it? In this book we seek to answer this question. We also explore some implications of the headlong pursuit of higher standards.

Can assessment play a more constructive role in the process of learning itself? Are there different kinds of assessment that should be being pursued if we are to equip young people for the world of the twenty-first century? What's in it for schools, teachers and pupils in terms of changed assessment practices? This book explores these questions from the perspective of both teachers and pupils.

Are schools and teachers using assessment to promote learning?

The answer, coming from a range of sources, suggests that while assessment practice has improved over the years, teachers could achieve still more if they used the information they gather about pupils' learning more effectively to plan and teach their lessons. Pupils' experience and

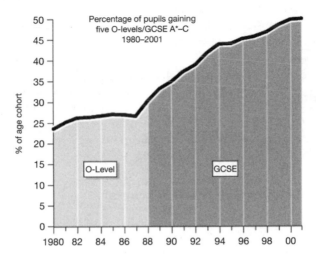

Figure 1.1 O-level and GCSE results (1980–2001)

Source: *Times Education Supplement* (23 Nov. 2001): 23

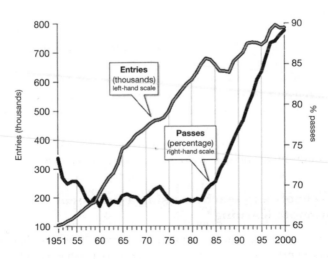

Figure 1.2 Ascent of the A-level (1951–2000)

Source: *Times Education Supplement* (23 Nov. 2001): 23

Figure 1.3 'Standards are rising' – are pupils becoming better learners?

understanding of assessment is an important factor in raising standards. While pupils are better at doing examinations what do they understand of the assessment they experience, and is the quality of their learning better?

Much of the material we draw on to answer these questions comes from a research project (the LEARN project) conducted during 1999 and funded by the Qualifications and Curriculum Authority (QCA). LEARN was designed to find out both how pupils viewed themselves as learners and also their views on the interaction between assessment and the learning process in school. A wide age range of pupils, from the early years of primary schooling through to the end of the sixth form, were interviewed. We describe the project in more detail in Chapter 3, but as later chapters of this book reveal, the results were startling. They show a picture of young people unclear about what they are supposed to be learning and why; unclear about their own strengths and weaknesses as learners; unclear about the feedback they receive from teachers about how to improve and progressively more dependent on the teacher to guide their learning.

Figure 1.4 'What do we have to do?' 'Don't worry – just do what I tell you.'

Is the current assessment regime asking the right questions?

If the findings of the LEARN project are a valid representation of pupils in schools in England today there is grave cause for concern. The pupils' responses suggest that despite achieving higher standards in formal tests, they are no more empowered as independent learners than before, indeed perhaps even less so, as the obsession with doing well continues to increase. Instead what emerges is that while pupils are better prepared to pass particular tests, they are not necessarily better equipped to use their knowledge and skills effectively in other contexts. Schools meanwhile, under pressure to retain or improve their place in published league tables and to meet specified achievement targets, have little time or energy to consider apparently more ephemeral issues concerning the nature of learning and pupils' engagement with it.

We hope that this book will challenge this mind set; that it will encourage teachers to consider the powerful role that assessment plays in the promotion or inhibition of learning and to take the longer view about the kinds of learning which will be important for pupils if they are to be equipped for life and work in the changed world of the twenty-first century.

How can learners be empowered?

What are the potential consequences of the growing emphasis on extrinsic motivation, on *trading for grades*, rather than the creation of learners who are empowered in more intrinsic ways? What is the impact on learning, particularly for lower achievers, of the fear and anxiety that the intense diet of external testing is creating? What are the implications for society of pupils who are less and less willing to take risks in their learning? How important are issues of creativity?

These are big questions and are perhaps best illustrated by the story of one pupil, Jenny, as described by her mother:

I notice the pain and anguish that my daughter, aged 7, is currently going through as she realises, much earlier than I did, how assessment goalposts can change. I think that my early and continued academic successes shield me from some of the social realities that she has to come to terms with much earlier in her life. Jenny is bright and thoughtful and a good reader (phew!). Unluckily she has some specific writing difficulties, partly because she genuinely doesn't care about how things are spelt (not a favourite with David Blunkett) and partly because she has enormous difficulty writing quickly and legibly. She is young for her age and my version is that this will develop. Although she is off the scales on the reading and mental maths stakes, her teachers this year have put her in the 'derrh brains' group, because she never finishes her work and it is often illegible. She is humiliated.

Throughout the infants school she was an achiever. She took part in plays, played the violin and the piano, was given certificates and awards for art, for being a good friend, for being a good musician, for helping catalogue the library etc. She even got a certificate in assembly for holding a *Blue Peter* bring and buy sale and she felt successful. Now she feels a failure. The goalposts have changed and she can only get a smiley face on her chart for two things – spelling and times tables tests. If the whole family busts a gut for the week she sometimes gets all her spellings right, but only once has there been a smiley face for maths. She writes it down wrong or too slowly.

Jenny has entered sullen adolescence overnight and partly I feel distraught for her, but listening to her work out the ludicrousness of the test culture and the boring and unadventurous place her school has become for her I also wonder if she has made an important discovery that will stand her in good stead. She knows she is still good at the things that used to be valued, she also knows that they are not important any more to school but that they are very important to us. As she recently pointed out to her intractably naive mother, 'It doesn't matter about understanding things in the juniors, just as long as we get them right. I mean there's no time to go into understanding stuff. That all takes ages and you have to have a go. In the juniors there's a lot less having a go and a lot more getting told things'.

This theme is taken up by David Almond, the author of the prize-winning children's book *Skellig* and himself a former teacher. Lamenting the stifling of creativity in schools he predicted that in 50 years' time:

the concentration on assessment, accreditation, targets, scores, grades, tests, profiles will be seen as a kind of madness. . . . The pedants are triumphant and go about their task of disintegrating our world . . . like medieval philosophers they debate the exact weight to be given to every fragment, 15% on this subject, 12.5% on that, 5.7% on the other. There's an arrogance at work. The arrogance that we know exactly what happens when someone learns something, that we can plan for it, that we can describe it, that we can record it and that if we don't do these things then the learning doesn't exist. The arrogance leads us to concentrate on a particular kind of work, noses to the grindstone treadmill kind of work, work that is observable, recordable and well nigh constant. So, . . . get kids into school fast. Get them assessed while they are in nappies. Get them going in literary clubs, numeracy clubs, lunch time learning clubs, holiday learning clubs. Holidays – let's cut them. School day – let's lengthen it. Homework – one hour, no let's make it two. Let's see them, children and teachers, work, work, work and let's get plenty of people watching them and recording them while they're at it. What would the assessors and recorders have made of Archimedes splashing happily about in his bath before he yelled 'Eureka!' What would they have made of James Watson snoring in his bed as he dreamt the molecular structure of DNA?

(Alberge, 1999: 8–9)

David Almond's personal view, as quoted above by Alberge, is supported by the findings of a major research study [the Primary, Assessment, Curriculum and Expectations (PACE) project] (Pollard *et al.*, 2000) that documented the impact of the National Curriculum and national assessment on pupils' learning in primary schools. The study concluded that:

the combined effect of recent policy changes in assessment has been to reinforce traditionalist conceptions of teaching and learning which are associated with a greater instrumentalism on the part of pupils. From this it can be argued that rather than acquiring lifelong learning skills and attitudes, the effect of recent reforms has been to make pupils more dependent on the teacher and less ready and able to engage in deep learning.

(Broadfoot and Pollard, 2000: 24)

But does this matter? As long as pupils are learning the curriculum that is being delivered to them, should we not be content that all is well in the world of education and assessment?

In the end it all depends what you mean by learning. In England, teachers have never defined their role simply as the transmission of knowledge to pupils. Their commitment has always been a more broadly based one of seeking to excite in their pupils a love of learning and of creating an environment in which this can happen. Now these traditional professional orientations are increasingly being underpinned by the recognition that a rapidly changing world requires new types of learning. The explosion of new learning opportunities already available through the world wide web and other forms of new opportunity requires each individual to develop the capacity to chart their own route, their own learning map, their own individual targets for learning. They need to be capable of choosing such options, of managing risk in a complex and unpredictable environment. In life, as in work, they will need to have the creativity to generate new solutions to problems and last but not least, they will need to have the self-reliance, the resilience, to fall back on their own resources in an increasingly fragmented world. In short, as Guy Claxton (1998) has put it, they will need to 'know what to do when they don't know what to do'.

If this is the vision of the future, it has significant implications for curriculum and teaching methods on the one hand, and for the orientation of students to their learning on the other. At its heart it requires pupils to become learners who are self-motivating and empowered within the learning process. As Steinberg has so trenchantly put it, 'no curricula overhaul, no instructional innovation, no change in school organisation, no toughening of standards, no rethinking of teacher training or compensation will succeed if students do not come to school interested in, and committed to, learning' (Steinberg, 1996: 194). The truth of this statement is the daily experience of every teacher.

What are we really assessing?

Learning is clearly a complex process. The sustained emphasis on changing teachers' classroom practices that has characterised government policy in recent years, as for example in the recent literacy and numeracy hours, has had the effect of obscuring equally important issues about how pupils learn and the factors that impact on that learning. As Sternberg has said:

> schools affect intelligence in several ways, most obviously by transmitting information . . . Perhaps at least as important are certain general skills and attitudes: systematic problem solving, abstract thinking, categorisation, sustained attention to material of little intrinsic interest and repeated manipulation of basic symbols and operations. There is no doubt that schools promote and permit

the development of significant intellectual skills which develop to different extents in different children. It is because tests of intelligence draw on many of those same skills that they predict school achievement as well as they do . . . We know much less about the forms of intelligence that tests do not easily assess: wisdom, creativity, practical knowledge, social skill and the like. . . . Despite the importance of these abilities we know very little about them, how they develop, what factors influence that development, how they are related to more traditional measures.

(Sternberg, 1996: 87–97)

Is it the case that important aspects of learning have been relegated to the sidelines because our traditional testing technologies only lend themselves to measuring a very small proportion of what children learn? How far should we agree with what Charles Handy calls the McNamara fallacy:

The first step is to measure whatever can be easily measured. This is OK as far as it goes. The second step is to disregard that which can't easily be measured or to give it an arbitrary quantitative value. This is arbitrary and misleading. The third step is to presume that what can't be measured easily really isn't important. This is blindness. The fourth step is to say that what can't easily be measured really doesn't exist. This is suicide.

(Handy 1994: 219)

Malcolm Ross, a leading protagonist for education in the arts, offered a similarly trenchant criticism of the effects of too much emphasis on measurement even before the advent of national assessment and the enormously increased policy profile of public assessment issues:

Assessment, more precisely examination, is rapidly becoming the sole objective, so it would seem, of education . . . Increasingly our education system at all levels is succumbing to the pernicious doctrine . . . a pestilence caught exclusively off managerial moguls. Emotional enfeeblement and moral degeneration could become the defining characteristics of our society by the turn of the century as today's schoolchildren take on the executive role . . . Those of us who resist the march of the assessors do so on the grounds that the loss of happiness is too high a price to pay for a spurious legitimacy.

(Ross 1986: ix)

These are strong words and many people would regard them as overly polemical. Nevertheless it is the case that countries around the world, not least many Asian countries, in which children achieve some of the highest standards in the world in conventional tests, are actively exploring new models of teaching and learning which they feel will better prepare students for the twenty-first century. So obsessed have students in these countries become with getting high scores in external examinations that their capacity for independent thought and creativity has been severely reduced. In the words of one newspaper headline:

"Exam culture is failing our students"
South China Morning Post (5 March 1999)

Is it time to question common assumptions about education and schools?

It would seem that it is time to question many of the established, almost taken for granted, assumptions about education and schools. As far as learning is concerned, John Abbott of the 21st Century Learning Initiative has provided a list of these assumptions, which includes the following:

- intelligence is largely innate, as is creativity
- as children become older they need more formal instruction
- learning is dependent on direct instruction and extrinsic rewards
- learning is seen as being strictly logical, objective and linear
- real learning is accomplished in formal settings and is measurable
- learning is dependent on class time and the technology of paper, pencil and textbooks.

(Abbott, 1999: 1–12)

It is not difficult to see the way in which these assumptions are built into contemporary education policy and indeed much of our current classroom practice. These deeply entrenched assumptions about the process of teaching and learning have recently been overlaid by what might be called the assessment panacea. There can be little doubt that governments have lighted on assessment as a powerful means of forcing schools to implement policy and of raising standards through target-setting and league tables. The assumptions informing this policy panacea can be described as follows:

- that assessment is a neutral instrument which, with progressive refinement, is capable of measuring an individual's level of achievement objectively
- that there are standards that can be measured
- that it is necessary and desirable to assess institutional quality according to externally defined performance indicators
- that the punitive use of league tables and other publicly shaming devices will help to drive up educational performance
- that decisions concerning curriculum (inputs), pedagogy (process) and assessment (outcomes) should be centralised.

Unfortunately we appear to be throwing out the baby with the bath water by focusing on measuring performance (summative assessment). Whilst a great deal has clearly been achieved in recent years in promoting higher expectations and greater rigour in the teaching and learning process, the effect has arguably been to obscure equally important and perhaps even more fundamental aspects of the relationship between assessment and learning. It is these more fundamental aspects that form the subject of this book.

Using assessment to promote learning

Our aim is to document and explore how schools can use assessment more effectively to promote learning (formative assessment) and hence to fulfil the original goals of the National Curriculum as expressed, for example, in the Task Group on Assessment and Testing Report of 1988, which provided the foundation for the current system for national assessment.

Promoting children's learning is the principal aim of schools. Assessment lies at the heart of this process. It can provide a framework in which educational objectives may be set and pupils' progress charted and expressed. It can yield a basis for planning the next steps in response to children's needs. It should be an integral part of the educational process, continually providing both 'feedback and feed forward'. It therefore needs to be incorporated systematically into teaching strategies and practices at all levels.

(DES/WO, 1988: paras 3 and 4)

However, the laudable aspirations of the members of the Task Group on Assessment and Testing (TGAT) have not, it seems, been achieved in subsequent years. In its recent review of secondary education in England, for example, OFSTED reiterated its commitment to the role of assessment in promoting learning in stating, 'Overall, the purpose of assessment is to improve standards, not merely to measure them. Although the quality of formative assessment has improved perceptibly it continues to be a weakness in many schools' (OFSTED, 1998: 91–2).

Despite this, the growing prominence of assessment as an aspect of educational activity has helped to fuel a growing body of interest among both teachers and policy makers concerning the potential of formative assessment. It is only relatively recently that the concepts of formative and summative assessment have become familiar in the world of education. The distinction between them is an important one. We suggest:

- Formative assessment is assessment which is part of the process of teaching and learning – *assessment 'for' learning.*
- Summative assessment is the process of summing up or checking what has been learned at the end of a particular stage of learning, whether this is a module or a GCSE course – *assessment 'of' learning.*

This book uses 'formative assessment' and 'assessment for learning' interchangeably to mean the same thing. Similarly 'summative assessment' equates to 'assessment of learning'. The first is an essentially dynamic process in relation to learning, the second does not impact directly but clearly impacts indirectly on the learners' sense of success and failure and their evolving identity and self-concept.

Most of our existing assessment procedures, for example tests, exams, marks and grades, have evolved in relation to the needs of summative assessment. Although formative assessment has always been a part of the teaching and learning process, for instance in the comments teachers have made on pupils' work, it is only very recently that it has become an explicit focus for attention. Thus it is not surprising that the educational community is much more confused about what constitutes formative assessment and how it may best be conducted than it is in relation to more familiar forms of assessment practice.

As a recent QCA survey of headteachers, senior managers and class teachers from primary, secondary and special schools on formative assessment revealed (Neesom, 2000), there is considerable enthusiasm among teachers for the perceived benefits of formative assessment. Teachers recognise the importance of having whole-school policies that encourage an assessment dialogue between teachers and learners, identify good practice and recognise the shared responsibility for learning with learners. For teachers, formative assessment can provide valuable feedback and feed forward for effective planning and class-room intervention, both individually and collectively with their colleagues. For pupils, formative assessment skills are perceived as crucial for helping them manage their own learning development. Further, the survey revealed that teachers feel that the tremendous pressure to improve pupils' performance devalues their formative assessment practices. There is a pressing need for more support for teachers to develop a shared professional view of what constitutes formative assessment and for training in relevant techniques. In short, progress in achieving the aspirations of the original TGAT ideal of assessment for learning is being inhibited by a policy climate which puts enormous emphasis on only one kind of learning outcome.

What is the emotional impact of assessment?

Significant as these issues of priorities are for teachers in terms of how they conduct assessment practices, arguably even more significant is the impact of assessment on the learner. As Robert Reineke has pointed out, instruction touches the mind, assessment touches the heart. It is perhaps one of the most overlooked but profoundly important truths of education that learning includes both intellectual and emotional components.

Assessments, formal or informal, considered or casual, intentional or not, powerfully affect people, particularly students. The assessment climate that students experience is a critical component of instruction and learning. Students' assessment experiences remain with them for a lifetime and substantially affect their capacity for future learning. . . emotional charge is part of the character of assessment information.

(Reineke, 1998: 7)

As everyone has experienced, assessment can lead to elation or dejection, fear or excitement, but is rarely neutral. Ask any adult to reflect on their best and worst moments at school and they will usually recount an assessment episode. In many cases these episodes are still painful many years later. Psychologists have long recognised the role of emotion in learning, in terms of self-esteem, motivation, attribution theory and so on, but this recognition does not seem to have spilled over into the world of educational practice. As Sylvester points out, 'by separating emotion from logic and reason in the classroom we have simplified school management and evaluation but we have also then separated two sides of one coin and lost something important in the process. It's impossible to separate emotion from the important activities of life. Don't even try' (Sylvester, 1995). The centrality of emotion within the learning process is well demonstrated in the comments by the pupils interviewed as part of the LEARN project. It is almost beyond belief that the role of emotion in learning, and in assessment in particular, has received so little attention within both educational research and educational policy making.

A news item in the *Observer* (Summerskill, 2000) reported the findings of a study concerning pupils' self-esteem and its impact on learning as a major new discovery, namely that measured levels of self-esteem at age 11 were more important predictors of success in future life than intellectual ability. Pupils who are confident and experience a sense of achievement, it seems, are more likely to profit both from schooling and to be successful in life more generally.

The experience of the classroom is a highly emotional one for pupils. There is an abundance of telling evidence from students themselves that this is so. The PACE project, for example, has documented the growing anxiety of pupils as they go through primary school and the pressure to get it right increases. It documents too the particular chagrin experienced by pupils who find themselves faced with repeated experiences of failure. Studies of secondary pupils too by Jean Rudduck (Rudduck *et al.*, 1996) reveal a rather similar picture of growing alienation, disaffection and boredom among pupils who realise that they are not likely to be among the winners in the external assessment system.

Good teachers know that this is so. They know the importance of encouragement and of a sense of achievement. They know the damaging effect of even a casual remark on the bottom of a piece of work. They strive to create a positive learning climate for their pupils. This book is about building on such experiences, on the insights that can be gained both from educational research and from good practice to provide more general guidance about how assessment can be used to promote learning. It is a book that challenges the received wisdom of current education policy making and the status it gives to summative external assessment.

Conclusion

In this chapter we have argued that teachers and schools need to think of assessment in a new way, a twenty-first century way. The key features of this new way are:

- a focus on the use of assessment to empower pupils as learners
- a recognition of the impact of classroom assessment on the pupil's sense of self, on expectations, on motivation, and on confidence
- that assessment should provide guidance to both teachers and pupils about what needs to be learnt next
- that assessment should embody an approach to teaching and learning in which the development of long-term dispositions is more important than short-term performance
- an approach to assessment that challenges the educational community to develop new approaches and techniques that support the educational ambitions of the twenty-first century.

The scale of the problem and what schools and teachers can do about it is the subject of the chapters that follow.

ACTIVITIES

1 Reflect on your own experience of assessment. How has it effected your sense of self, expectations, motivation and confidence?

2 Discuss within your department/school how the results of a recent assessment (homework, test, extended task, role play, etc.) can be used to help pupils know what needs to be learnt next.

3 What are the opportunities and barriers to using assessment for learning in your classroom/school?

2 Can assessment for learning raise standards?

The simple answer to this question is YES! Research evidence suggests that by using assessment for learning (formative assessment) effectively teachers can improve grades significantly.

> Our education system has been subjected to so many far-reaching initiatives which, whilst taken in reaction to concerns about existing practices, have been based on little evidence about their potential to meet those concerns. In our study of formative assessment there can be seen, for once, firm evidence that indicates clearly a direction for change which could improve standards of learning. Our plea is that national policy will grasp this opportunity and give a lead in this direction.
>
> (Black and Wiliam, 1998a: 19)

Improving standards, not merely measuring them

The theme of this chapter comes from an OFSTED report that stated, 'Overall the purpose of assessment is to improve standards, not merely to measure them. Although the quality of formative assessment has improved perceptibly, it continues to be a weakness in many schools' (OFSTED, 1998: 91–2).

Over the past ten years the introduction of a national testing system in England has had a profound effect on schools and classrooms. As Dylan Wiliam (2000) suggests, the effect is a powerful demonstration of the truth of Goodhart's law. This law was named after Charles Goodhart, a former chief economist at the Bank of England, who showed that performance indicators lose their usefulness when used as objects of policy. In the current educational context this means that while year-on-year 'test' results may increase this may not indicate that pupil learning is better, merely that pupils are better at taking the test.

In Chapter 1 we argued that schools need to take a broader view of assessment if pupils are to be helped to become lifelong learners. This chapter discusses the tensions between the different purposes of assessment (formative, summative, evaluative and diagnostic) and defines some of the terminology used throughout the book. We give examples of the research evidence that shows how assessment for learning (used interchangeably with the term formative assessment) can raise standards and improve children's learning, both now and in the future. These examples are contrasted with the evidence of learning based on measuring performance (assessment of learning) that has dominated education in England and Wales over the last ten years.

The purposes of assessment

Assessment for learning is of course only one of several purposes of assessment. Commonly a four-fold classification of the purposes of assessment is used.

1 *diagnostic*, to identify pupils' current performance
2 *formative*, to aid learning
3 *summative*, for review, transfer and certification
4 *evaluative*, to see how well teachers or institutions are performing.

While this classification is useful in helping teachers focus on the different purposes of assessment it can also be a barrier. Any assessment could be used to provide data for most or all the different purposes listed above. It is not the assessment itself that is diagnostic, formative, summative or evaluative but the way that the information collected is used. As Dylan Wiliam and Paul Black (1996) suggest, 'These terms are therefore not descriptions of kinds of assessment but rather of *the use to which information arising from the assessments is put.*'

Table 2.1 Some definitions of assessment terminology

Diagnostic	*Indicates how current performance differs from expected performance. Can be used to identify specific problems that a pupil may be experiencing.*
Formative	*An assessment that helps pupils learn; results in actions that are successful in closing the gap between current and expected performance.*
Summative	*An assessment that is used to certify or record end of course performance or predict potential future attainment; the final product of a unit or course; an examination grade.*
Evaluative	*Assessment information that is used to judge the performance of schools or teachers; league tables.*

There has been much debate as to whether a single assessment system, such as that proposed by TGAT for the National Curriculum (DES/WO, 1988) can serve all these functions. One important factor, as Dylan Wiliam (2000) points out, is that 'very few teachers are able or willing to operate parallel assessment systems – one designed to serve a "summative" function and one designed to serve a "formative" function'. He argues that to enhance pupils' learning, teachers need to find ways to integrate the diagnostic, formative and summative functions of assessment and not be driven by the evaluative function.

It is also important to recognise that even the most objective assessment method will only give a partial view of the pupil being assessed and any inferences made and judgements reached should always be tentative and subject to alteration in the light of further data. There is a long tradition in England of teachers labelling pupils as high or low ability, when they are actually talking about attainment against a relatively narrow set of academic learning objectives and an ability by the pupil to 'play the assessor's game'. Some pupils are seriously disadvantaged by the current assessment system, while others benefit.

Validity, reliability and manageability

At this point we need to consider three important underpinning and sometimes competing concepts of assessment – validity, reliability and manageability. It is helpful to understand the differences between them and the tension that results from trying to balance them within any

Table 2.2 Definitions of validity, reliability and manageability

Validity of assessment method	*To what extent does an assessment measure what it sets out to measure?*
Reliability of assessment	*How consistent is the measurement of results between different teachers, between different test situations, etc.?*
Manageability of assessment	*Can the assessment be conducted without too much disruption to normal teaching?*

one assessment. This tension is well illustrated by the story of National Curriculum assessment in England and Wales during the 1990s, where teachers were pulled in different directions by shifting emphases as assessments were developed.

The early Key Stage 1 (KS1) classroom-based tasks

In 1988 the TGAT report suggested that formative, summative and evaluative functions could be combined in the new National Curriculum assessment system being described for 5–16-year-olds in England and Wales. This 'new' assessment system was intended to increase the *validity* of the judgements by using a range of assessment methods, often arising out of classroom tasks. However, the desire for 'valid' tests soon got lost in a quagmire of manageability and politics. The initial attempts to have 'valid' classroom-based tasks for KS1 children (such as the 'floating and sinking' tests) ran into problems because although they allowed children to demonstrate their knowledge and understanding they took a long time to administer and there were questions about the reliability of their administration by different teachers. They were rapidly abandoned to be replaced by cheaper, more 'reliable' pencil and paper externally set tests (Daugherty, 1995: 35–48).

The transition from KS2 to KS3 – the validity and reliability of the data

In 2000 David Blunkett (then Secretary of State for Education and Employment) highlighted his concerns about the transition of pupils from KS2 to KS3 and the disappointing lack of progress for many in

KS3. While there may be many factors that account for the lack of progression – such as cultural, emotional or developmental change – one factor also present is questions about the validity and reliability of the tests or tasks used. It is clear many KS3 teachers do not use information passed to them from KS2 to guide them in their teaching; instead they use a number of other measures or trust their own judgements. To justify not using KS2 information many question the validity and reliability of the levels data. They ask questions such as:

- Does a level 3, 4, 5 mean the same at KS2 as at KS3? There are questions about both validity and reliability implicit in this question. The curriculum is different in the two key stages and the tests take different forms. Children are different ages and teachers may interpret the levels differently, all of which could influence the 'score' a child achieves.

- Are standard test or teacher assessment scores reliable? As discussed later, any assessment only has currency if it is trusted and felt to be reliable. Often teachers seem to place more trust in measures other than National Curriculum tests, because they 'know' the problems there are in achieving reliability in National Curriculum tests.

- What does a level 3, 4, 5 mean different pupils can do? The number covers such a wide range of attainment that it has little meaning when comparing pupils who may 'know' different things and have a variety of skills.

- How can I handle all the information provided for me? Busy teachers are often concerned about the amount of data they have to get to grips with and whether they have time to really understand what it tells them about pupils' learning.

Thus schools face a number of dilemmas when deciding how best to use assessment to raise standards. This chapter looks at the promise, reality and challenges of both formative and summative assessment and provides compelling evidence that formative assessment can raise standards significantly.

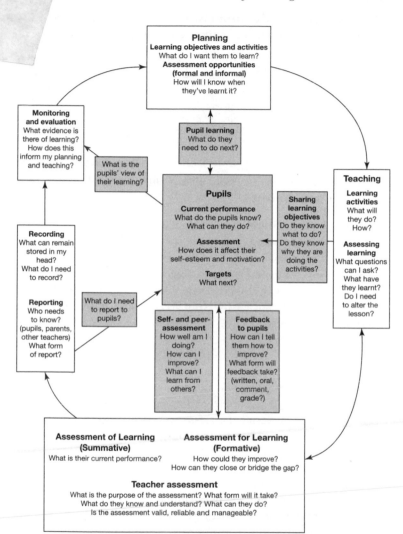

Figure 2.1 Teaching, learning and assessment

The promise, reality and challenges of formative assessment (assessment *for* learning)

In 1997 the Assessment Reform Group (ARG), a group of assessment experts, commissioned Professors Paul Black and Dylan Wiliam to review the research literature on formative assessment. ARG was concerned that the time and effort that teachers had put into assessment following the introduction of the National Curriculum was focused almost exclusively on assessment of learning (summative assessment).

What does the research show about the power of formative assessment?

The research evidence in Paul Black and Dylan Wiliam's report (1998a: 33) clearly showed that assessment for learning can raise standards. By altering their assessment practice in the classroom, teachers had helped pupils improve their performance significantly, which if translated into everyday classroom practice could mean a gain of two to three grades at GCSE. The gains reported in the research came about where teachers used assessment to help pupils learn, not just to measure what they had learnt.

What are the key factors in assessment for learning?

The report identified a number of key factors that helped improve learning through assessment. These are listed below and will be examined in more detail later in the book.

Assessment for learning:
- is integral to teaching
- involves sharing learning goals with pupils
- aims to help pupils know and recognise the standards they are aiming for
- requires adjusting teaching to take account of the results of assessment
- is underpinned by confidence that every pupil can improve
- requires a recognition of the profound influence assessment has on the motivation and self-esteem of pupils

- needs the provision of effective feedback to pupils so they can recognise their next steps and how to take them
- involves pupils in self-assessment
- encourages the active involvement of pupils in their own learning
- involves both teacher and pupils reviewing and reflecting on assessment data.

Case studies of assessment for learning

These key factors are illustrated by four examples, taken from Black and Wiliam's paper, that show how a focus on formative assessment led to gains in learning.

Example 1: Mastery learning, motivation and self-esteem

A teacher in the USA recorded his experience with over 7000 students over about 18 years of using *mastery learning* with his classes. His pupils' learning was geared towards achieving mastery of the work they were doing rather than accept some lower partial success. Pupils were regularly tested and had to achieve scores of 90 per cent before they could progress to the next topic. Over time, the effect of this was that pupils' efforts were focused on achieving these high scores and they moved on more quickly. Their scores were higher than those of other comparable pupils and they developed more positive attitudes towards learning and school.

Clearly, this is an example where the teaching and assessment were interlinked and informed each other so it was more than just adding some tests to an otherwise unchanged teaching programme. The pupils were clear about the goals and standards to be achieved, the shift in responsibility to the pupils was important to their motivation and self-esteem, as was the teacher's belief that all pupils *could* succeed.

Example 2: Using self-assessment as a learning tool

A group of teachers of mathematics in Portugal were trained in the use of self-assessment and implemented the ideas with their pupils. When pupils' achievements were compared with a control group who had not used the self-assessment methods, they showed a much greater gain.

Figure 2.2 Clarity of goals leads to success

This was strongest in a group of 8/9-year-old pupils but also present in a group aged between 10 and 14. The self-assessment methods used were teaching pupils how to understand the learning objectives and assessment criteria for their work, allowing them to choose their learning tasks and using tasks which allowed them to assess their own progress. (See Chapter 4 for more about self-assessment strategies that can be used in the classroom.)

As with Example 1, this type of programme required a wide-ranging examination of the teaching methods used – these classrooms were quite different places as a result of these methods. Again the pupils were being required to take much greater responsibility for their learning than might normally be expected.

Example 3: Largest gains for low achievers

A programme of science teaching incorporated *reflective assessment* into some pupils' experiences. All the pupils undertook a programme of experimental work, but one group of students was introduced to the use of reflective discussion as a self- and peer-assessment tool. A control group engaged in discussion but without this reflective component. The testing of pupils' learning at the end of the programme showed gains for the experimental group over the control group, but perhaps most significantly, those showing the highest comparative gains were the lowest-scoring groups. In other words, the benefits of this form of learning were most pronounced for the lowest achievers.

This is an important finding, given the current focus on the under-achievement of a 'tail' of pupils. This type of structured reflection on their learning seems to be a way of boosting their achievement substantially and increasing their motivation and self-esteem, by involving them more actively, helping them clarify the goals and giving them self-assessment strategies.

Example 4: Self-evaluation – focus on learning, not performance

This was a study of four groups of 9/10-year-old pupils who carried out a programme of work on fractions. For two groups the emphasis of the teaching was on *learning goals* (in other words learning how to solve the problems) and for the other two groups the emphasis was on *performance goals* (or just solving them). One group for each type of goal engaged in frequent self-evaluation, while the other did not. The group with the performance goals that did not engage in self-evaluation came out lower in terms of skills and motivation than the other three groups.

This showed that of the two focuses for the research – goal orientation and self-evaluation – self-evaluation was the most important. A further study, which simply compared two groups working with the two different goal orientations, showed that the learning-goals orientation led to greater learning gains.

So there are two messages here: the first, already seen in other examples, that self-evaluation is an important part of making learning effective; the second that an emphasis on learning rather than performance can lead to improved outcomes. Given the push for 'performance' in terms of examination and test results in schools at the moment, perhaps this is a result that should be considered carefully.

What are the benefits of developing formative assessment?

The evidence provided here shows that assessment for learning can help pupils make significant gains in learning. One important consequence of this can be improvements in behaviour as pupils (and teachers) begin to believe they can succeed. Successful assessment for learning is not something extra; it is part of everyday teaching and learning, helping teachers and pupils reflect on the progress being made. Teachers who have successfully introduced it into their classroom practice have started small, tried out one or two strategies that they have adapted to their own context, and once those have been successful they have extended and developed them.

Some challenges for teachers in developing assessment for learning

The four examples demonstrate that there are complex interconnections between learning, teaching, assessment and motivation. The initial challenge for teachers is to clarify for themselves what they understand by 'formative assessment' and to decide how they can make initial (small) changes to their practice that will help pupils actively engage in their own learning, help them be clear about their current performance and decide what they need to do next.

A second challenge is to recognise that teacher expectations have an important effect on pupils' learning and to look for strategies that have a positive impact on motivation and learning. In all the examples the teachers believed their pupils could succeed and the improvement in the lower attainers' achievements in Example 3 is a particularly powerful illustration of what can be achieved.

A third challenge is that teachers may initially find formative assessment time-consuming. The introduction into the classroom of formative assessment strategies, such as sharing objectives and evaluating learning (self-assessment), may appear to reduce the time for teaching. Teachers may need to spend more time marking work and feeding back comments, but experience suggests this issue disappears later.

A fourth challenge is learning how to collect and interpret data formatively. Actually any assessment can be formative if it is used not just to categorise a child as a 'level 3', 'level 5', 'A*' or 'F' but also to identify how performance can be improved. Dylan Wiliam (2000: 4) in describing the assessment cycle suggests, 'all four functions of assessment require that evidence of performance or attainment is elicited, is then interpreted, and as a result of that interpretation, some action is taken'. The assessment becomes formative if the information collected is used by the teacher or the pupil in the learning process.

The final challenge is to recognise that any change will take time to implement and will need support from colleagues, parents and policy makers. Change does not happen overnight and teachers need to be able to experiment and share ideas and find out what works for them in their context.

More detail about the examples, and others which illustrate how formative assessment can improve learning, can be found in Paul Black and Dylan Wiliam's review in *Assessment in Education* (1998b).

What is summative assessment (assessment *of* learning)?

Summative assessment is a snapshot judgement that records what a pupil can do at a particular time. It is concerned with providing information about a pupil in a simple, summary form that can be used to review progress, can be passed on to a new teacher or school or can certificate the pupil's achievement in a formal way. This function probably dominates most teachers' views of assessment. These individual achievements are also used to evaluate teacher, school or LEA performance. The current emphasis in England and to a lesser extent in Wales appears to be 'If it moves, measure it', with baseline assessments, end of module assessments, key stage assessments and external examinations, to mention but a few.

The promise, reality and challenges of summative assessment

> The combination of both pressure and support is driving improvement just as it is doing in America's most rapidly improving states . . . In schools up and down the country there has been a dramatic shift in the last two years or so. They are all sharply focused on results and how to achieve them.
>
> (Blunkett, 2000)

Policy makers in England have increasingly focused on summative assessments as a key mechanism of accountability. The positive effects of this focus have been that many teachers' understanding and use of assessment have improved, expectations of pupils' achievement levels have risen year on year, pupils' measured 'standards' are steadily rising, teachers' implicit notions of 'fixed ability' have been challenged and schools have been made accountable for the progress pupils have made. Another possible benefit is that pupils practise passing tests throughout their school career so that when they take 'high stakes' examinations they are more familiar with them. ARG has argued that the National Curriculum tests might have a more positive value for the children if they were not at the end of the key stages, thus giving teachers opportunity to take some action to reduce areas of weakness, and if there were a profile for each pupil rather than an overall level. But these points depend on the breadth and curriculum validity of the assessment. For example, it appears that the more broadly based KS1 tests generally have more positive learning effects than the more narrowly focused KS2 tests.

However, there are negative effects of summative assessment. These include achievement levels rising merely because they are being measured, teachers feeling that the 'effort' required to achieve the ends is not worthwhile and the introduction of an exam culture into lower primary years narrowing the curriculum and placing pressure on pupils. This can result in children 'failing' at an early age which can lead to an attitude of learned helplessness. Schools can become uncomfortable for children because there are higher expectations and dull work, where the emphasis is on coaching them to answer test questions with formulaic responses. Teachers may feel deskilled in their day-to-day work and use of assessment in the classroom, because these areas are not valued. Finally the tests may lack validity because what is tested does not truly reflect what children know, understand and can do.

The promise – does summative assessment help individual pupils learn?

The answer has to be: maybe. The key questions here are how is the information about performance on the assessment communicated to the pupils, parents or other teachers? and does the information help pupils' future learning?

Communicating by a report on a pupil

There is a real tension for teachers in providing this information. The more detailed any report is the longer it takes to prepare and read, but there is no guarantee that it will be used effectively by the person/ institution receiving it. How can pupils and parents be encouraged to read and follow through comments? How can schools guarantee that information is passed on effectively both within and between schools? Schools therefore have to consider what the purpose of any report is, decide the most efficient method of collecting and recording data so that it is used effectively to set targets for individuals and then ensure that the targets are followed through.

Communicating by mark or grade used for certification

Everyone has experienced externally produced and marked tests and examinations that classify and record the overall achievement of a pupil in a systematic way. The commonest form is the classification (mark or exam grade) where a range of disparate assessment information is reduced to a single score. Such classifications tend to be of little help in future learning but may have a profound affect on an individual's self-esteem and motivation. For example, three pupils receive grades A, D and F in an examination. On receiving the piece of paper that tells them their grade, what information do they have about their individual performances? Will they use this to help them with later learning? Almost certainly not, because this summative examination is a rite of passage, an end in itself, that merely certifies their learning performance at that time. However, it will affect their self-perception – 'I'm an A, D or F person' (whatever that is) at this subject – and this may affect their approach to learning in future assessments.

The reality – are 'standards' rising?

The evidence suggests that year-on-year examination grades are rising. However, the concept of a 'standard' is problematic. Any summative assessment has to gain social meaning for it to be useful. Dylan Wiliam (1996) argues that 'standards' are socially constructed, rather than representing something precisely measurable:

Examination results are 'social facts'. Like bank notes they depend for their value on the status that is accorded to them within a social system. As foreign currency markets have found out to their cost, it is not possible to create comparability by fiat. Similarly, all attempts to define 'standards' or 'equivalence' independently of the social setting in which they are created have failed, and indeed are bound to fail. Two qualifications are comparable only to the extent that there are people who are prepared to believe they are comparable.

(Wiliam, 1996: 304)

However, gaining social meaning doesn't mean it is any use in helping someone learn – it is merely a shorthand record of their learning at that point in time, that may be useful in opening (or closing) doors and helping them progress (or not) to the next phase of their education or life. In fact, despite the many attempts to 'standardise' results, many external 'formal' grading systems such as GCE A-levels or degree results only have currency because they are socially valued. At GCSE it is generally accepted that grades A*–C are 'good', although good is not clearly defined for most people.

Some challenges for summative assessment

Can 'standards' in different qualifications be compared?

In England and Wales, GCSE and A-level grades have a currency that is recognised by employers or higher education. Newer qualifications such as GNVQ may be viewed with more suspicion because there is less 'understanding' of what a foundation GNVQ pass, merit or distinction means in terms of attainment. Until newer qualifications become more commonly recognised and valued they tend to be viewed as having a lower status.

The National Qualifications Framework

The latest attempt to rationalise and standardise the assessment system in England and Wales has been the introduction of the National Qualifications Framework (NQF). The NQF is an attempt to provide

Table 2.3 National qualifications framework

Level of qualification	General	Vocationally related	Occupational
5	higher-level qualifications (see note)		level 5 NVQ
4			level 4 NVQ
3 advanced level	A level	vocational A-level (advanced GNVQ)	level 3 NVQ
2 intermediate level	GCSE grade A*–C	Intermediate GNVQ	level 2 NVQ
1 foundation level	GCSE grade D–G	Foundation GNVQ	level 1 NVQ
entry level	certificate of (educational) achievement		

Source: QCA (2002)

Note: responsibility shared with the Quality Assurance Agency (QAA) for higher education

an understandable and comparable framework that rewards achievement along different routes (academic and vocational).

This initiative attempts to increase both the reliability and validity of national assessment. It seeks to broaden the areas assessed, to use a wider range of methods and to enable comparability between different specifications. However, comparability is problematic between academic and vocational routes. Is a level-3 qualification (equivalent to A-level) comparable between two very different types of qualification, such as A-level food technology or GNVQ catering? Comparison is even more difficult between two very different subjects such as physics and tourism.

The benefits and dangers of 'high-stakes' testing

George Madaus (1988) suggests that there are benefits to the sort of nationally driven 'high-stakes' assessment regime currently being experienced in England and Wales. If the skills are well chosen, the tests truly measure them, and the goals of instruction explicit then teachers and pupils can focus their efforts on well-defined targets. Such a regime also generates clear and uniform standards; easier and more objective accountability at all levels and provides concrete information on how well schools are doing for the public.

However, there are negative and unintended consequences as well. Madaus framed a number of principles that are worth considering:

1   The power of assessment depends on how it is perceived by the users. If they believe it to be important it will be. One effect of this can be that governments use testing to show that they are doing something to raise standards.

2   The more important a quantitative social indicator becomes, the more likely it is to distort the processes it is supposed to monitor. Thus when schools are set targets to achieve they are likely to focus their efforts in specific ways, for example by providing extra coaching for borderline grade C–D candidates at GCSE to boost the number of pupils achieving A*–C grades or entering more candidates for four GCE A-levels (three plus General Studies) to boost individual point scores.

3   If important decisions are presumed to be related to test results, teachers will teach to the test. Scores may rise without skills improving. There is currently some debate as to whether the methods used in the literacy hour are actually improving the quality of reading and writing even though scores for basic skills are improving.

4   In every setting where test results are important, a tradition of past examinations develops which eventually *de facto* defines the curriculum.

5   Teachers pay particular attention to the form of questions and adjust their instruction to teach exam technique.

6   When test results are the sole or even a partial arbiter of future educational or life choices, society tends to treat test results as the major goal of schooling rather than a useful but fallible indicator of achievement.

7   A high-stakes test transfers control over the curriculum to the agency that sets or controls the exam.

Can regularly measuring performance raise standards?

It is clear that merely measuring something doesn't result in change. Alongside the measurement there has to be some action that helps pupils learn. By measuring performance and publishing the results, schools have been made more accountable and are forced to implement the many new initiatives that government has introduced. In some cases there have been spectacular successes with measured results improving significantly. However, the measurement itself does not improve performance; it is the educational changes underpinning it that are important. As Paul Black and Dylan Wiliam (1998a) suggest in the quote at the beginning of this chapter, many initiatives introduced by government are untried and their effectiveness is unknown. Contrasted with this is the research into formative assessment that clearly shows standards can be raised.

At the individual level assessment can motivate individuals and focus the mind if it is believed to be important. Many pupils are motivated to work when they know that the assessment of a piece of work is going to help them gain a certificate. They are far more likely to practise, revise or take more care in their writing or preparation for 'high-stakes' tests. A consequence however is that the test, assignment, task or examination defines the content to be learnt. For instance, teachers and pupils will often use previous years' examination papers to 'guess the question' and define the areas most likely to be examined. In almost all these situations teaching to the test occurs and the curriculum is narrowed.

On a more positive note there is evidence that testing can bring about constructive and positive curriculum change, as the introduction of the GCSE examination in England and Wales showed. Being forced to introduce new assessment methods, to find ways of assessing what pupils knew, understood and could do resulted in some important changes in teachers' practice, once they had got over the initial problems of an unfamiliar system. These changes broadened the types of assessment used. The evidence from the introduction of both GCSE and National Curriculum assessment systems is that real change only occurs where teachers are willing to involve themselves fully in understanding the principles behind the change and modify it to suit their own context. This takes time and requires support.

Some key issues in raising standards through formative assessment

In the final part of this chapter we return to the main theme of this book: that formative assessment can empower pupils as learners. It is important to remember that assessment, teaching and learning are interlinked. An assessment episode can result in pupils learning, inform teachers about what pupils can and can't do and also be used to inform future planning. Teachers can and do assess pupils all the time as part of their teaching, not just through formal episodic methods. Pupils should be helped to understand their own performance and what they need to do next.

Remembering purpose

Perhaps the most important point underpinning this chapter is that teachers should consider the *purpose* of any assessment. One purpose of assessment can be to improve learning, which is very different from the purpose of measuring the learning that has taken place. Having clear purposes (learning intentions) will be explored further in Chapter 6.

Weighing pigs!

It is sometimes said, 'the pig doesn't get fatter just by being weighed'. Formative assessment, as a tool to raise standards, is an exception to this rule. It is about finding ways of weighing the pig that *do* help it get fatter. Without stretching the analogy too far, it is about involving the pig in its own fattening and about constructively using the information from the scales to help us decide on feeding programmes. All of which says that it is not the simple, isolated act of measuring that matters, but the complex network of decisions and actions that links assessment, learning and motivation.

Using evidence

An absolutely fundamental shift in teachers' practice in recent years has been a shift towards *evidence*. There are now enormous quantities of data available about teachers' own pupils, comparisons with others and what is expected. The formative assessment agenda can make this an opportunity rather than a strait-jacket. Ways can be found to use this mass of data to make decisions which are led by learning needs and not just by 'performance' goals.

'Knowing' individuals

Assessment of individuals is a powerful tool in understanding them better and thereby being able to focus the teaching that they need more effectively. An example of this is given by Mary James in her work with Non Worrall (James, 1998). Non describes an assessment intervention made with a pupil with a history of disruptive behaviour. The observations of this pupil and her peer group allowed Non to make targeted interventions to support her learning and to improve the climate in the classes she was in. The point is that this action could not be undertaken without accurate and appropriate information about the pupil concerned. The assessment cycle of elicitation, inference and action means teachers can work with their pupils to determine effective actions and to support their learning. This can be a time-consuming activity but has rewards in its widespread effects, not just for the pupil concerned.

This last point is linked to an idea that is fundamental to the work of all teachers – the basic information we have and use every day relating to all our pupils. Partly this grows up over time and partly it is the result of specific information gathering, which is done to give a foundation of knowledge of what will and what won't work with individuals or classes. Peter Airasian (1996) calls these 'sizing up' assessments and alerts teachers to the fact that by their very nature they are partial and imperfect, as are all assessments. The trouble is, it is possible to feel that a pupil is 'known' well despite only ever meeting him or her in a very narrow set of contexts and in a very specific relationship. However, if these limitations are recognised, this 'teacher knowledge' forms an important part of the learning relationship between the teacher and all their pupils.

Target-setting

A final aspect of assessment for raising standards without which this section would not be complete is that of *target-setting*. Schools are beset with targets of all varieties at the moment, and they can provide a very useful focus for specific action. Remember the acronym SMART?

Targets should be Specific, Measurable, Achievable, Relevant and Time-related (or sometimes some other similar set of words). What is important is to keep sight of the purpose of setting targets and to use them to achieve this rather than as a stick with which teachers can be beaten when they fail to achieve the impossible. Target-setting will be discussed further in Chapter 3.

Conclusion

Looking back over this chapter, it is worth considering the overall message from the research. There is strong evidence that assessment for learning will raise standards and this book looks at some of the strategies that schools can employ. However, it is not possible to have all the answers in a ready-made package. Schools and teachers will need to work with government, LEAs, inspectors and Higher Education Institutions (HEIs) on finding methods that work in different contexts. It is important to recognise that small initial steps are necessary, that change takes time and needs the support of a wide range of people. As ARG argued:

> It is important that a focus on assessment for learning is not seen by teachers as adding to the expectations of them, but as integral to the already well understood project to raise educational standards. That must be spelled out wherever possible in official statements and echoed in the attention given to assessment for learning in other contexts such as survey reports from OFSTED and other national inspection agencies within the UK. It is our belief that many teachers and schools already do appreciate that effective practice in the use of assessment within classrooms and across schools is essential if we are to achieve real and lasting improvements in educational standards.

(ARG, 1999: 12)

Many schools and teachers are aware of the issues and are already working to develop effective assessment for learning. More detail is given about some of the key areas later in the book, but the point to make here is the power and potential of formative assessment. It is not just a woolly idea – it is a proven, successful strategy for raising standards.

ACTIVITIES

1   Using research evidence

The four examples of formative assessment in this chapter offer different views on how formative assessment can improve learning. As you read them, consider how they relate to your own experiences and how you might go about achieving some of these gains in your own teaching.

2   Identifying these features in our own teaching

What opportunities do you give pupils to engage in some of the types of activities described in this chapter?

How can you introduce some of these features of formative assessment into your teaching?

More importantly, what implications does this have for other aspects of your teaching? What else will have to change so that these ways of working will be an integral part of your teaching rather than a 'bolt on'?

3   Using assessment data effectively

Consider your end-of-key-stage teacher assessment. What information does it provide for:

- Formative assessment purposes? How could you use the information gathered to aid pupils' learning?

- Summative assessment purposes? How could you use the information gathered to review progress, transfer information within or between schools or for certification?

- Accountability purposes? How might the information be provided to parents or the wider public?

Do you feel that this assessment package can provide information for all these purposes or are some elements better for particular purposes?

3 Can current assessment practice be improved?

> Assessment remains the weakest aspect of teaching in most subjects . . .
> Despite much energy expended on assessment, nearly all whole school
> assessment policies have weaknesses or gaps which are reflected in
> corresponding weaknesses in the assessment practice of teachers.
>
> (OFSTED, 1998: 88–9)

In many classrooms the issue is not that teachers aren't assessing
enough, but that they aren't using the information they collect to help
pupils learn. We therefore ask you to consider one fundamental question: *Do you, as a teacher, know enough about what your pupils know, understand
and can do to help them learn?*

This chapter develops the case for the power of formative assessment to raise standards and the need for a recognition that teaching,
assessment and learning are interlinked. As OFSTED have said:

> Good practice requires an understanding of the reasons for assessment and the systems and structures adopted in the school. It
> entails regular and purposeful marking of pupils' work; consistent
> and accurate judgements of pupils' attainment; effective use of
> day-to-day assessment to provide pupils with feedback and to
> inform the setting of targets; and manageable systems for recording
> pupils' progress.
>
> (OFSTED, 1998: 88)

Are schools using assessment to help pupils learn?

While the steady improvement in test and examination scores over the last few years in England and Wales is to be welcomed, it does not necessarily mean that learning is better, merely that teachers are better at training pupils for these particular tests. The area where there is most room for improvement is formative assessment. In considering how assessment can be a positive force for learning, we ask four questions:

- How effectively do schools deal with assessment issues?
- How do pupils view and use the information they are given by teachers?
- How does assessment affect the motivation of low- and under-achieving pupils?
- How can schools promote fairness and equity in assessment practice?

How effectively do schools deal with assessment issues?

Teachers often groan when assessment is discussed. It's not seen as 'sexy' – more of a chore to be endured. The many changes that have occurred in the assessment system in England and Wales over the last few years have often left teachers feeling confused, that their professional judgement is no longer sufficient and that they are being swamped by the requirements of an externally imposed system.

What are the main issues for schools to consider?

In Chapter 2 we discussed the important research carried out by Paul Black and Dylan Wiliam (1998a) on assessment for learning. Their paper also outlines three sets of issues arising from the current testing regime. The findings apply not just to England and Wales but are mirrored in a number of other countries where research has been undertaken.

1   There is a mismatch between teachers' stated beliefs about effective learning and the assessment methods they use.

2   There is clear evidence that there is a negative side to assessment which results in many students under-achieving or failing to have their knowledge, skills and understanding recognised.

3   There is a danger that assessment purposes are being swamped by the managerial role of the assessments.

What do schools need to consider for each of these issues?

Is there a mismatch between teachers' beliefs and actions?

The mismatch between teachers' beliefs and the assessment methods they use is highlighted by the research evidence that shows that assessment to support learning is not effective because:

- Teachers' tests encourage rote and superficial learning; this is seen even where teachers say they want to develop understanding – and many seem unaware of the inconsistency.
- The questions and other methods used are not discussed with or shared between teachers in the same school, and they are not critically reviewed in relation to what they actually assess.
- For primary teachers particularly there is a tendency to emphasise quantity and presentation of work and to neglect its quality in relation to learning.

The implications are that schools and teachers need to consider whether their practice matches their rhetoric. Do the methods used really promote the sort of learning that will encourage pupils to become lifelong learners?

Does assessment have negative effects on learning for some pupils?

The research evidence suggests that assessment will have a negative impact on pupil learning where:

- The giving of marks and the grading functions are overemphasised, while the giving of useful advice and the learning function are underemphasised.

Figure 3.1 Are assessment methods successful?

- Pupils are compared with one another, because this focuses pupils' attention on competition rather than personal improvement. As a result assessment feedback teaches pupils with low attainment that they lack 'ability', so they are demotivated, believing they are not able to learn.

These two findings are highly significant and will be discussed further later. Many schools appear to be reluctant to abandon the use of grades despite the evidence that they do not aid learning.

Is the managerial function of assessment more important than the learning function?

The research evidence suggests that:

- Teachers' feedback to pupils often seems to serve social and managerial functions, at the expense of the learning function.
- Teachers are often able to predict pupils' results on external tests – because their own tests imitate them – but at the same time they know too little about their pupils' learning.
- The collection of marks to fill up the records is given higher priority than the analysis of pupils' work to discern their learning needs. Furthermore, some teachers pay no attention to the assessment records of previous teachers of their pupils.

The research findings about schools' effectiveness in dealing with assessment issues suggest that two areas may need to be considered. First, the dominance of the summative function of assessment in many schools has produced benefits for some children but costs for others. Second, teachers are less confident in diagnosing learning difficulties or suggesting actions that may help pupil learning, than they are in collecting marks that record attainment.

How do pupils view and use the information they are given by teachers?

The pupil's view of assessment has been less well researched. The findings presented here are largely derived from the LEARN project

(Weeden and Winter, 1999), introduced in Chapter 1. The research was commissioned by the QCA and was carried out in early 1999. Over 200 children of different ages (from year 3 to year 12) were interviewed to gain insights into their perceptions of themselves as learners and their understanding of how they think they learn best. The interviews provide a thought-provoking insight into pupils' views of assessment, how they think they approach learning and their motivation.

The pupils interviewed ranged from year 3 (7–8-year-olds) to year 13 (18–19-year-olds), which allowed both similarities and differences over the age groups to be identified. Through semi-structured group and individual interviews pupils were asked about their understanding of their course and the sort of assessments they did; the researchers then attempted to indirectly identify motivational factors. The most important themes to emerge are summarised below. Year groups are given in parentheses after pupil quotes. The project findings are interesting because, while they can't attempt to give definitive answers, they do give a different perspective on the relationship between teaching, learning and assessment.

How well did pupils understand what they had to do?

All age groups were dependent on their teacher to guide their learning.

> Miss wrote on board and we copied it down and then had questions to answer. (Y6)

At all ages pupils had a good surface understanding of individual tasks, but less sense of the 'big' purpose of the task – they tend to do what the teacher tells them.

> She'd give us a booklet which tells us what we'll do. It's got marks for each bit. (Y9)

> I try and get it neat with no gaps in – in case you wanted to give it to someone. The teacher said try and get no gaps in it. (Y9)

> It's half of me doing what I want to do on it and half the teacher. (Y9)

Lower attainers were most reliant on teachers and more likely to be confused. At GCSE level there was evidence that there was a split between the information given to students. Higher attainers were allowed to be more autonomous while lower attainers were not told so much (thereby being kept more dependent on their teachers).

> We don't know how it (coursework) will be assessed but we know what to do – they give us sheets and stuff. (Y10)

> When we work on coursework the teacher says we should look through it and see what's right. But sometimes I don't know what to do. (Y10)

> In English we get a coursework plan saying generally what we've got to include. (Y10)

What understanding did students have of how their work would be assessed?

Pupils were more likely to report being rewarded for limited criteria such as punctuation, spelling and effort rather than quality of learning. Older children had a better understanding of assessment criteria but the most frequently mentioned by all age groups were effort, presentation and accuracy. Pupils were aware that there were different criteria for different subjects but many were also confused by the differences.

Assessment criteria identified by younger pupils included trying hard, being neat and accurate; by year 6 this had extended to good handwriting, spelling, punctuation and showing working (in maths). They were aware that there were different criteria for different subjects and there was clear evidence that teachers emphasised certain aspects of work – metaphors, adjectives, structure (in reports of science investigations – introductions and conclusions).

> No-one thinks much of scribble or big writing. (Y3)

> It's one of my best because my handwriting is joined up neat. (Y3)

> Smiley faces are for working hard, neat handwriting, spelling the date right. (Y3)

> My writing was good, most of it was joined up. (Y6)

At GCSE effort, presentation and accuracy were still mentioned but there was a clearer understanding that there were significant variations between teachers and subjects (English required imagination while maths needed working to be shown). Planning, method and technical aspects were also identified.

> Yes, I think I asked the right kind of questions but when I wrote the bit about it at the end I think I could of done more detail – put more things in what I did. (Y10)

> We did a story and Miss said it was very good – my punctuation and paragraphs. (Y10)

> What they look for is understanding information. (Y10)

GNVQ students suggested that effort was still important but they were also clear about the meaning of each performance criterion, range statement or evidence requirement. However, they seemed less clear about the 'big picture', how they were doing in relation to achieving a pass, merit or distinction. At GCE A-level some students had a much clearer idea of the criteria and were able to comment on the structure and content of their work.

> I'm unsure about how I'm doing in relation to pass, merit or distinction. (GNVQ)

> Mostly on style, the amount of points, how you've expressed those points and how you've given your point of view towards those points. (A level)

What factors did students report affected their motivation?

It was possible to identify a different variety of motivations: mastery or performance orientation; learned helplessness; intrinsic or extrinsic motivation. All of these terms are explored further later in this chapter.

Pupils had a lot to say about why they worked in some subjects and not others. What emerged was a complex network of internal and external motivators that interact within individuals. However, a common thread for many was performing well.

> If I don't work my friends will get ahead so I work even if I'm not in a good mood. (Y3)

> I works really hard – cos I wants to do good. (Y6)

The prospect of working for examinations had a positive effect for some.

> This year, if you miss lots of school it's going to really hinder your education to get through your exams. (Y10)

Post-16 students tended to take more responsibility for their learning because they had chosen the subject and because their goals were clearer.

> Sometimes I do more work than I used to because I actually want to do it. (GNVQ).

> I want to get to where I want to be in ten years' time so I see getting good A level results and a good degree as part of that. (A level)

What goals did pupils have?

Pupils had both long- and short-term goals, often linked to assessment or certification.

Long-term goals

Some students had clear ideas about their futures and the relevance of school.

> Science, English and maths are most important – all jobs use a bit of that. (Y9).

> I want to be an architect and go to college. I need my Art and my English and Maths, because you've got to work out points and stuff. (Y9)

Others, meanwhile, could see little point.

> If I want to be a model none of it will be important. (Y9)

> I want to be a midwife – we don't do nothing on babies. Science has got a lot to do with it but not a lot. (Y10)

Higher-attaining students on GCSE courses were more focused on their futures, often with clear ideas about courses or jobs they intended to go on to post-16.

I'd like to be a chartered engineer – there's lots of directions I could go. I think the more grades you get above C grade then the more options you have. I think maths, English and science cover a lot of the job aspects. (Y10)

GNVQ students often had clearer ideas about their future plans than A-level students. The strong vocational focus of the GNVQ work helped to reinforce students' ideas while A-levels left students with a more open agenda.

I'd like to do entertainment at Pontins or somewhere like that. I've got work experience planned out there. (GNVQ).

I chose my A levels on the basis: ones I was good at, ones I was interested in and ones I could maybe make a career out of. (A level)

Short-term goals

As well as the longer-term goals described above, short-term goals were important in motivating many students. In year 3 this might have been to do with keeping up with friends or not staying in at lunch time. During year 6 the KS2 tests were a factor for many students. Lower attainers in year 9 were in some cases quite inward looking and had few goals. Affective factors were very important here – 'moods' and teachers making work interesting. Other year 9 students had some awareness of KS3 tests but did not seem to be particularly concerned to work towards them.

The influence of national tests is felt at an early age:

SATs are going to be hard – no play. (Y6)

and some students were clearly aware of their position in the hierarchy:

I'm trying to work hard to get into the top set. (Y6)

For students in examination groups, GCSE, GNVQ and A level, there were short-term goals built into the structure which helped guide them, but the longer-term goals of examination success were strong.

I've organised myself more and set my mind on certain things – make sure coursework and homework come first. It's only a few years you've got to knuckle down and then you've left school and you can decide what way you want to go. (Y10)

What was the pupils' view of targets?

When targets are set for pupils they can be quickly forgotten and failure can result if there is no follow-up. In the LEARN project when target-setting was discussed with pupils, most had only the vaguest idea of the process. What pupils reported was that targets were set, but they were seldom monitored or their achievements recognised:

> 'In our reports they set us targets.' *'Will you look back at these?'* 'I'm not sure if we will. I probably won't do it myself but we might do it in a lesson, I don't know.' (Y10)

> One time after our reports we were given a sheet and had to write down targets for ourselves. In our organisers we've got a special page for targets where we write down what our targets are and a review date. I've only ever done it once I think, that's when we first got it. Basically we don't get told to do it. (Y9)

> 'We've got a targets page in our organiser.' *'Do you use it?'* 'No. I don't use my organiser for that sort of thing. You don't look at it as much. You don't have time to do it at school. I would if they told us to do it at school. (Y9)

> 'Yes I think we have them – I can't remember where they come from. (Y9)

> I don't think they write about the old target, they just write a new one. (Y10)

> In year 10 they don't really bother with targets. In year 7 they're quite strict. Our tutor does give them out. I've achieved most of them – stop talking and sit away from my friends and get on with my work well. (Y10)

What has the target-setting process offered these pupils in terms of improving their learning? They report the erratic nature of the process and considerable dependence on the teacher. There seem to be mechanistic procedures in place in these schools, which are sometimes followed and sometimes not, and the link with any real learning is far from clear. The only pupils who had positive comments to make about targets were those who were self-motivated enough to set and monitor their own targets independent of any school system.

What did pupils identify as reasons for success in school work?

Pupils identified three reasons for success in school work – effort, ability and opportunity to learn. Younger pupils were more likely to attribute success to effort and opportunity and made little mention of some pupils being intrinsically more able to achieve than others. Only a few higher-attaining pupils in years 3 and 6 mentioned ability as a factor while in year 9 and later it was more likely to be lower attainers who mentioned ability as a factor. The influence of gender on effort was not an area analysed in detail, but some pupils (girls) felt boys were less motivated and more likely to misbehave. There was little clear evidence that they felt gender influenced ability. Throughout the years up to year 11 'working hard' was seen as the most important factor in achieving success. Post-16 students had the most balanced view, attributing success to a mixture of the two factors of effort and ability.

> People are different – everyone's good at something. (Y3)
>
> They listen and work hard. (Y6)
>
> Some have read more books. (Y6)
>
> It's just genetics. (Y9)
>
> Cos they're brainier and they work harder. (Y9)
>
> Boys don't do well because they mess around. (Y10)
>
> I do think you have pupils who are more gifted than others. (A level)

These comments give some insight into pupils' perceptions of motivation and equity. The rest of this chapter looks at these two issues in more detail and in particular considers how the links between assessment, teaching and learning cannot be divorced from pupil self-image and cultural background.

How does assessment affect the motivation of low- and under-achieving pupils?

> The performance of pupils in public examinations has improved steadily over the last five years. . . . However this overall increase masks very unequal rates of improvement. The increase for the lowest performing quarter of pupils has been very much less than for others.
>
> (OFSTED, 1998: 16–17)

Schools are rightly concerned about the poor motivation of low- or under-achieving pupils, because of its impact on teaching, learning and behaviour. Motivational research has been extensively developed since the 1980s and there are two themes of particular relevance to assessment practice at the institutional and individual level. How does assessment affect motivation? and can schools make a difference?

How does assessment affect motivation?

At the institutional level the organisation of schools can result in totally different experiences for pupils, which may have serious consequences for motivation. For instance, when a school 'differentiates' its pupils for organisational purposes or as a result of assessment, this affects social relations within the pupil culture. Termed 'polarisation', the basic process is that some pupils come to favour the school more, and to try harder at their studies, whilst others become dispirited and may become more deviant. Such divisive processes are particularly likely to emerge as assessment processes become more overt and high-stakes.

Setting, option choices and allocation to different levels of tiered GCSE papers are all examples of differentiation that may well lead to pupils adopting progressively different attitudes to school. In what is essentially a multiplier effect, schools publicly promote the achievements of their high attainers (with half an eye on boosting enrolments), whilst also developing increasingly sophisticated systems for behavioural control and reluctantly contributing to a steady rise in pupil exclusions.

There is little doubt that national assessment procedures have long-term effects on pupils. For many pupils, these effects will be positive, in that the quality of teaching and learning will be enhanced. However, some pupils will experience negative effects which could both damage their self-image and self-confidence and have other divisive effects for our society as a whole.

At the individual level motivation is a vital component of learning, and it is important for teachers to understand how pupils' motivation is linked to assessment, self-esteem and feedback. Paul Black (1998) quoting Sylva's (1994) research on early primary children suggests that learners' feelings about themselves develop at an early age. Sylva identified two main types of children:

Mastery children
- are motivated by the desire to learn
- will tackle difficult tasks in flexible and reflective ways
- are confident of success, believing that they can do it if they try
- believe that you can improve your intelligence
- if they see another hard-working child, they will say 'she must be interested'

Helpless children
- are motivated by the desire to be seen to do well
- seem to accept that they will fail because they are not clever enough
- believe that if something seems to be too hard there is nothing they can do about it
- tend therefore to avoid challenge
- do not believe they can improve their intelligence

Sylva (1994) cited in Black (1998: 133–4)

These two categories do not appear to be related to 'intelligence' and can be influenced by schools, particularly through effective feedback (which is discussed further in Chapter 5).

Somewhat similar categories of motivational types are found in the work of Colin Rogers (1994), who has drawn both on the writing of researchers in North America such as Carol Dweck and his own research in Britain. However, he extends the idea of motivational styles by suggesting that learners adopt different motivational strategies according to the context. This idea challenges commonly held 'western' views of 'innate fixed ability', enabling teachers to find ways of supporting low- and under-achieving pupils. He compares the notion of motivational style to 'styles of dress' that vary according to the occasion;

successful adapters respond to their understanding of the context (wedding, walking trip, night out). The important idea here is that successful adapters have a clear understanding of what is needed.

Colin Rogers suggests that learners can be classified into three motivational types, but that they can and do move between the types according to the context. In describing these three motivational types we have also suggested how assessment for learning can raise achievement for all of them.

'Mastery'-oriented pupils

Mastery-oriented students are intrinsically interested in 'knowing', will be motivated to learn and will develop strategies that help them do this. Teachers can all give examples of pupils like this, who when asked to investigate a problem do so with enthusiasm and skill, coming up with interesting and original ideas. Someone who is academically low-achieving may be outstanding in another context such as music or sport partly because they have the motivation to practise and develop their skills. Mastery-oriented learners will often implicitly recognise how they can improve their work. Teachers need to tap into their intrinsic motivation by providing feedback on performance that encourages, supports and challenges.

'Performance'-oriented pupils

Performance-oriented pupils are less concerned with the task and more concerned with being 'seen' to do well, thus boosting their own self-esteem. This can reduce their motivation in certain situations, and because they don't want to be seen to fail, they find strategies that place the blame on others or factors beyond their control. Again teachers will recognise the pupils who account for their failure to complete homework by blaming the printer – which didn't work, or the dog – which chewed it up, rather than either their lack of effort or their lack of understanding of the task. Research has shown that where pupils can be encouraged to focus on the quality of the task outcome, rather than the quality of their performance, learning can be more successful.

Teachers need therefore to find ways to comment on the quality of the task outcome, not the performance of the person. Separating the two can be problematic and pupils who have invested a lot of effort into a task will often feel undervalued by comments that the teacher did not intend as criticism of the person. This can be as simple as the comment 'try harder' – if a pupil feels they have tried as hard as they can, but the final product is still poor, they may feel they are the failure, not the piece of work. However, giving unmitigated praise is not the answer – pupils should be helped to understand notions of quality and of what is achievable, and to develop their own critical skills.

Learned helplessness

The final group of pupils have a history of academic failure and have developed an attitude of 'learned helplessness', so that they fail to engage successfully with the work. Teachers may 'label' them as lacking ability, with the result that they may not be provided with opportunities or appropriate challenges. They are often a major problem socially and behaviourally within the school. Schools are increasingly trying to find ways of helping them to be successful, maybe by breaking tasks down into smaller, more manageable stages, or making the curriculum more relevant to their needs so that they can break out of the pattern of repeated failure.

To conclude, in the classroom context, the teacher can help all pupils become more 'successful' by ensuring they all know what they are expected to achieve. This means having clear and appropriate learning intentions and sharing them with all the class. One way this can be achieved is by providing 'advanced organisers'. Advanced organisers were proposed in the 1960s by a cognitive psychologist, Ausubel, who showed that when learners have a clear model of the learning task it helps them sort and classify the content they will be studying.

Assessment and motivation

The current assessment regime of regular testing, from baseline assessments on entry to school through to school-leaving examinations, is in danger of labelling pupils by ability from the earliest age. Students who are successful in the current assessment regime may adopt a mastery-oriented strategy with associated positive effects on their learning. They are less likely to be deterred by setbacks or failures. Unsuccessful students may adopt the learned-helplessness or performance-orientated motivational styles, with the result that their learning is less successful.

An important message for teachers is that ability is not innate and fixed, that attainment and motivation are context specific and can and do change. As a result it is important not to assume that any individual pupil lacks 'ability', but instead to consider how they can be helped to move to a position where they feel more confident of success.

Can schools make a difference?

There are a number of ways that learner motivation style can be changed, such as target-setting, self-assessment and feedback. Target-setting will be explored here while Chapter 4 considers self-assessment and Chapter 5 feedback.

Target-setting – reducing the negative impact of assessment on motivation

The testing regime has created a challenge – we have more information than ever about children's performance and teachers spend a large part of their time collecting and recording this information. The challenge for schools is how to use this information as effectively as they can to raise standards and motivate pupils. One common approach is target-setting, although as already indicated in this chapter many pupils find the target-setting process of limited use because it is rarely followed up effectively.

Target-setting can be done at national, LEA, school, class and pupil level. For instance, in 1997 the government announced national targets for literacy and numeracy in England requiring that by the year 2002

- 80 per cent of 11-year-olds would reach level 4 in English, and
- 75 per cent of 11-year-olds would reach level 4 in mathematics.

The DfEE in its document *From Targets to Action* (1997) suggested a five-stage development programme for target-setting at school level. This was led by five key questions and it is worth considering how these questions could fit into the learning of individual pupils as well as being a way of examining a school's systems.

The questions are:

- How well are we doing?
- How well should we be doing?
- What more can we achieve?
- What must we do to make this happen?
- What have we done?

These questions give teachers a way of examining, with pupils, where they are, where they want to be, how to get there and how well they have succeeded in getting there.

How can teachers make the target-setting process meaningful and positive?

The challenge for teachers is to use target-setting effectively to motivate pupils, particularly those seen to be underachieving. As Chapter 2 suggested, measurement alone will not achieve this aim, but formative assessment is useful because it focuses on diagnosing difficulties, making judgements about the quality of answers and suggesting actions that will raise performance.

Shirley Clarke (1998) makes the point that, for pupils, target-setting makes most sense if it works up from their achievements rather than down from school-level goals. Targets need to be real and focused on each individual's needs. She gives examples of small focused targets that are close to each pupil's present performance. These can be easily monitored and new targets developed as the previous ones are achieved:

- try not to reverse your bs and ds
- know your number bonds to 10
- write in sentences when answering comprehension questions
- proof-read for spellings.

If these targets are written on cards which pupils refer to whenever they are working on the relevant topic, they will have real meaning and effect and not be lost in a formal system inaccessible to the pupil. They are also more manageable for teachers since they are not hidden in books or filed away to be referred to infrequently. The overall progression of targets for the whole class can be identified in medium- and long-term planning.

One of the big issues with target-setting is how to make it effective and manageable. One way has been suggested above but teachers and schools might consider other ways that the data they collect about individual pupils' achievements can be used more effectively in their day-to-day work.

How can schools promote fairness and equity in assessment practice?

If the achievement of all pupils is to be improved we need to be sure that assessment practice promotes fairness and equity. This is an extremely important, but complex, topic that can only be briefly touched on in this book. Much of the research is derived from summative assessments, particularly formal examinations, but teachers will find that many of the issues are relevant to formative assessment and in particular to how they help pupils prepare for examinations.

What do we mean by 'equity'?

There is a broad consensus that our society should be 'open' and 'fair', but what exactly does this mean? 'Equality of opportunity' for people from all social groups is often contrasted with 'equality of outcome'. Equality of opportunity patently does not exist within the current British education system where inequalities exist as the result of a multiplicity of factors which even a supposedly 'equal' starting point can do little to offset. The debate over entry to Oxford and Cambridge for pupils from comprehensive schools illustrates one way that inequalities of opportunity must exist where resources are limited. Choices are almost bound to be somewhat arbitrary when a small number of equally qualified youngsters have to be selected from a large number of applicants.

On the other hand, if we believe that all social groups have the same inherent potential, then perhaps, in the long term, we should be aiming for equality of outcome. Yet the unique qualities of people are also to be celebrated and it is unlikely that we want to produce a bland, equal homogeneity. Caroline Gipps and Patricia Murphy (1994) offered the term 'equity' to by-pass these dilemmas and they endorse a 'spirit of justice' in which 'assessment practice and interpretation of results are fair and just for all groups'. Although still somewhat vague, perhaps such commitment is the only realistic position to take?

Is there equality in educational outcomes?

The OFSTED review of secondary education certainly didn't think there was equality: 'Certain groups of pupils perform far less well than others, and than might be expected of them. The under-performance of boys is a matter of serious concern, as is the fact that pupils from some ethnic minority groups often achieve below their potential' (OFSTED, 1998: 9).

Gender

A study by the Equal Opportunities Commission and OFSTED in 1996 (Arnot *et al.*, 1996) showed how girls outperformed boys at ages 7, 11 and 14 in English and were more successful at every level and in almost every subject at GCSE (the exception was physics). At that time these differences disappeared at A level, but increasingly the evidence suggests girls are outperforming boys here as well. However, teachers should remember that there are bigger differences between high and low achievers than there are between boys and girls. Not all boys are low-achieving and not all girls high-achieving. Inspection evidence suggests that about a fifth of secondary schools are 'weak' in meeting the needs of one gender or the other, though very few schools explicitly discriminate against either gender.

Social class and ethnicity

Unlike gender the evidence about educational performance by ethnicity and social class is more limited since to date this data has not routinely been collected. The evidence regarding social class is that there has been a very consistent and strong relationship with academic achievement: in general the higher the social class, the higher the achievement.

There are also distinct differences regarding ethnic origin. A study by David Gillborn and Caroline Gipps (1996) found that, compared with previous research more than ten years earlier, there were:

Figure 3.2 Equality in gender performance?

- generally higher levels of achievement that were continually rising
- improving levels of attainment among ethnic minority groups in many LEAs
- dramatic increases in performance of some groups even in LEAs with significant poverty.

However, they also found that African Caribbeans tended to perform less well than whites, whilst some Asian groups tend to do as well, or better, than both other groups. Evidence from the Youth Cohort Study

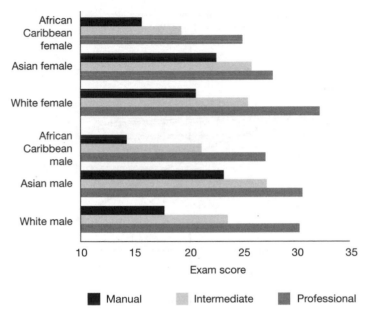

Figure 3.3 Average exam scores by ethnic origin, gender and social class (England and Wales, 1985)

Source: Gillborn and Gipps (1996: 17)

(Figure 3.3) provides an unusual data set of all these factors, and shows that in 1985 the strongest influence was social class. Schools will need to examine data from their own schools carefully to identify the patterns.

Why do these differences occur and what action can schools take?

The reasons for differential performance between the genders are complex. Changing attitudes to the role of women and their careers appear to have been important in raising girls' performance, while key factors contributing to boys' under-achievement appear to be some boys' lower motivation, more negative attitudes to school and their relatively poor ability to organise themselves and their work.

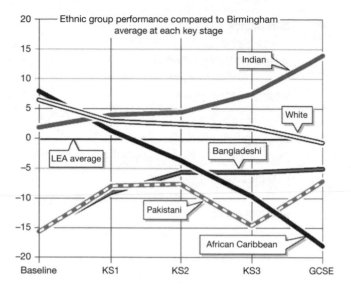

Figure 3.4 The long, hard road to disaffection

Source: *Times Education Supplement* (3 Mar. 2001)

The OFSTED review of secondary education suggests that:

> Schools and LEAs have become increasingly conscious of the differential performance of ethnic minority pupils, and some have developed specific strategies to raise their achievement. A starting point has frequently been the closer evaluation of data to identify the specific patterns of achievement in a school or LEA area.
>
> (OFSTED, 1998: 31)

Figure 3.4 shows how Birmingham LEA has used performance data to record the relative patterns of achievement of different groups of pupils. As John Hill, director of statistics, says, 'You've got to ask the question: what's happening (he indicated the infant – junior divide) to disengage a significant number of black kids, predominantly boys' (*TES*, 3 March 2001). This sort of data challenges simple conceptions of ability and highlights issues of motivation and alienation. Schools can make a difference by not accepting under-achievement and devising specific strategies for their context. OFSTED suggests:

> Such data can be useful in targeting initiatives and resources. General strategies include homework clubs, often run by language support teachers, which can make a major contribution to improving pupils' confidence and attainment. Similarly, the use of target setting and personal action plans can provide pupils with manageable learning steps with periodic review used to ascertain whether the targets have been met. Some specific projects targeted at African Caribbean pupils seek to improve motivation as well as offering individual support.
>
> (OFSTED, 1998: 32)

Are our forms of assessment equitable?

Ultimately, this seems most unlikely. The issue can be approached in many ways. For instance, Michael Apple in 1989 suggested distinguishing between 'curricular' and 'assessment' questions which might be asked with regard to different social groups. Thus:

- Whose knowledge is taught? Whose knowledge is assessed?
- Why is this knowledge taught in this particular way to this particular group? Are the form, content and mode of assessment appropriate for different groups and individuals?
- How can the histories and cultures of different social groups be taught in responsible and responsive ways? Is this range of cultural knowledge reflected in definitions of achievement?

These are very difficult questions, but the point to be clear about is that it *is* the case that different forms of assessment *do* produce differences in measured attainment and *can* be manipulated to adjust these outcomes. Assessment practices are therefore not 'objective' in any absolute sense: they measure what they are designed to measure. They are socially constructed, and to some extent, so is the performance or capability of the pupil.

How can outcomes be manipulated to improve performance?

An important question here is: should assessors try to manipulate outcomes, for instance to try to 'improve' boys' performance? The answer surely has to be that deliberate manipulation should be avoided, but that teachers should attempt to ensure that all pupils have the opportunity to demonstrate their achievements.

There are many ways in which unintended differences in assessed performance may occur, an issue which is closely linked to that of validity.

- The *form* of an assessment instrument may affect some pupils. A number of studies have found for instance that multiple choice response questions favoured boys and coursework tasks girls.
- In terms of the *content* to be assessed, ethnic, social and cultural background, as well as gender of pupils, will affect how meaningful a task or question is to pupils and therefore whether their performance in the assessment reflects their real understanding.
- The *social contexts* in which assessment activities are carried out have also been shown to impact on performance, with administrative procedures being a more specific example of this factor.
- A further issue of great significance concerns the *expectations* of significant others, such as teachers, peers or parents. These affect performance indirectly, through their influence on the self-confidence of the pupil.
- However, the influence of expectations may also be felt very directly through the *access*, or lack of it, to assessment at particular levels. Tiered examinations restrict access to certain grades for some pupils because they are not entered for the relevant tier in the first place. Low expectations by teachers are regarded as a much bigger problem than high expectations.
- *Marking* practices are also vulnerable to teacher expectations. If, even unintentionally, teachers classify pupils by 'ability', this classification may well become self-perpetuating.

This review of possible sources of distortion in assessment is clearly linked to many other issues of equity in education and is part of our argument that 'there is no such thing as an objective assessment'.

Teachers (and other stakeholders) should recognise that some forms of assessment can be misleading. The 'objectivity' of assessment practices cannot be taken for granted and teachers must be prepared to maintain an alert commitment to equity and the 'spirit of justice' when assessing pupils.

Some issues relating to equity

In this final section we describe some of the patterns relating to equity that have emerged from the research, along with possible explanations, and suggest some implications for teachers and schools to consider.

Entry patterns

Consistently there have been differential entry patterns for subjects at GCSE and A level. For instance, smaller numbers of boys took English A level during the 1990s but they performed slightly better overall than girls. The best explanation appears to be that this group that chose a traditionally 'female' subject were highly motivated.

At GCSE where there is tiered entry, entry patterns may be different. In 1994, 21,000 more girls than boys were entered for the intermediate tier. Mary James (1998: 202–3) suggests this either means 'that the performance of girls is underestimated in mathematics or that teachers enter them for the "safe" tier to protect them from anxiety. This will allow them to achieve the vital "C" grade whilst avoiding the risks of being unclassified.'

This suggests that schools and teachers need to carefully analyse their entry patterns and results for different subjects to identify possible areas where teacher expectations may be influencing entries. A more fundamental question may be to investigate what influences pupils' choice of different subjects. Are some subjects regarded more favourably by different groups – and if so, why?

Mode of assessment

The style of assessment appears to affect performance. For example, in 1999 boys performed better in the KS2 standard tests for English than they had in previous years. One of the reasons suggested for this change was the fact that previous years' tasks involved pupils reading and comprehending one longer piece of text whereas the 1999 text was in three smaller sections.

Summative assessments are changing their form and a wider variety of modes of assessment have been introduced. The evidence suggests that in order to allow all pupils to demonstrate their ability assessment needs to take a variety of different forms so that different learning styles are catered for. Patricia Murphy found in 1995 that boys and girls attend to different things in a task, and that neither response was wrong, just different. However, she also found evidence that one reason for the overall poorer performance by boys is that tests and examinations contain a greater verbal element than in the past, even in maths and science. Since language is an area in which boys have traditionally underperformed relative to girls this may cause significant problems of accessibility to the task.

The implications of these findings are that teachers need to consider strategies that increase accessibility to the variety of different modes of assessment for all pupils and not assume they will all respond in the same way. How can pupils be given clear guidance about the assessors' expectations for different modes of assessment?

Learning styles – style of response

Learning styles appear to have an impact on performance and the research findings suggest that it may be necessary to look carefully at how boys approach learning and find ways to help them cope better with assessment tasks. Patricia Murphy found that girls tend to use the sort of approaches to learning that current learning theories emphasise: relating knowledge to context in order to be able to apply it more widely, engaging in dialogue with other learners and the teacher in order to question and validate understanding and using collaborative approaches to learning. Boys on the other hand tend not to use these approaches.

The implications of these findings are that teachers need to be aware of the different learning styles that tend to be used by boys and girls and ensure that they prepare pupils appropriately for the variety of different assessments they are likely to encounter, recognising the different needs of boys and girls.

Figure 3.5 Appropriate learning style

Contextualising tasks

There is a lot of evidence to suggest that contextualising tasks can result in unintended bias. For instance, the growing trend towards contextualising tasks can result in boy-friendly or girl-friendly questions being set. The evidence of the Assessment of Performance Surveys in the 1980s suggests that all pupils perform better on tasks involving contexts they are familiar with, such as home and school. However, the contexts will vary, with girls responding better to personal and domestic situations and boys doing better on items about cars, buildings and machinery.

Teachers when setting their own tasks should consider how to reduce or eliminate contextual bias by using contexts that support different groups of pupils.

Ethnicity, social class and equity

What is clear is that differential performance is a complex interaction of factors with white girls from professional backgrounds tending to have the highest performance and African-Caribbean boys from a manual background having the lowest. Gordon Stobart and Caroline Gipps (1997) suggest the relationship between curriculum and syllabus content, teacher attitudes to pupils and minority ethnic groups, assessment mode and format need to be reviewed if fairness is to be achieved for all pupils.

Curriculum and assessment design is therefore important, and schools may want to consider how the curriculum and internal assessments are constructed so that they are relevant to all the pupils within the school.

Conclusion

The evidence from the different sources paints a somewhat gloomy picture. In many schools the emphasis on testing and accountability has resulted in the collection of masses of data about children's performance but a lack of time or understanding where the effective use of this information to enhance learning in the classroom is concerned. Often the information collected is merely used to record and report. Marking takes up many hours of a teacher's week but much of this time is spent checking that work has been completed rather than being more focused on identifying learning problems and helping pupils to identify problems for themselves. Pupils who are dependent on their teachers to guide them in their learning may not hear the message properly or only understand part of the story. As a result pupil potential can be wasted in our schools. Assessment has strong links to the complex issues of motivation and equity and teachers and schools should bear this in mind when preparing pupils for examinations and constructing internal assessments. In the rest of the book we will explore how different assessment strategies can raise performance.

ACTIVITIES

1   Are you and your school using assessment for learning effectively?

Consider Black and Wiliam's three sets of issues. How far do the statements reflect practice in your classroom/school?

Which one aspect of your assessment practice do you think most hinders your pupils' learning?

Devise an action plan that might improve your assessment.

2   Considering people's feelings when experiencing assessment

Join with a colleague and talk in pairs, each person taking it in turns to talk. First, each shares a personal experience from their childhood about which they felt positively. Second, each shares a personal childhood experience of being assessed about which they felt negatively. We suggest that each person talks, without interruption, for about five minutes.

When each person has shared their experiences, you should work together to identify the issues which were involved. Did any of the following come up: dignity, self-esteem, anxiety, humiliation, unfairness, pleasure, pride, recognition, affirmation?

Do you think the young people with whom you work in school have feelings now which are similar to those which you once had yourself?

3 Investigating the impact of assessment activity on pupils

Ask the pupils what they think about being assessed in your subject through coursework, testing or examination. An interesting way of doing this might be to set up a debate, with groups putting the case for, and against, particular forms of assessment.

Observation could provide another source of data. Watch the pupils carefully next time they are being assessed. How do they respond? Are some relaxed? Are others tense or anxious? Make some notes on your observations and let these accumulate over a week or so. Then review what you have found. Alternatively, if you want to obtain a large amount of material which can be analysed more systematically, you could ask pupils to express their views in writing.

As you gather data, look out for patterns. For instance, are there any differences between high achievers and lower achievers, between boys and girls?

Assessment is, necessarily, a means of differentiating between pupils. Thus, despite the fact that one major purpose of assessment is that pupil needs can be identified, it remains somewhat threatening. Consider, then, how you can both maintain constructive assessment activity and sustain the self-confidence of all the pupils in your class.

4 Improving pupils' understanding

Think of a recent assessment. How did you ensure the pupils knew what they had to do, how they would do it and what the purpose was? How can they be helped to have the 'big picture'?

5   Using assessment data

Discuss with a group of colleagues how test data is used in your school.

To what extent is it possible to predict performance 3 or 4 years later?

Does labelling pupils by ability lead to self-fulfilling prophecies?

Do Colin Rogers' categories of motivation help explain the performance of different under-achieving pupils?

4 How does self-assessment help pupils learn?

In Chapter 3 we suggested that current assessment practice could be improved in many schools if teachers used assessment information more effectively and didn't just mark to ensure that work has been completed. In this chapter we suggest that one, maybe radical, change teachers can make is to train their pupils to use self-assessment. The process of self-assessment helps them think about their own learning and understand it better.

The idea that self-assessment has great potential for raising performance was one of Paul Black and Dylan Wiliam's main findings (1998a, 1998b). They report that the research literature describes many successful innovations using self- and peer assessment, including examples of working with children as young as 5 years old. One of the crucial success factors in these strategies was that the innovations involved sharing with pupils an understanding of what they were aiming to achieve. As a result pupils became more committed and more effective learners; they learned to reflect on their own achievements and thus improve them. One of their major recommendations was: 'For formative assessment to be productive, pupils should be trained in self-assessment so that they can understand the main purposes of their learning and thereby grasp what they need to do to achieve' (Black and Wiliam, 1998a: 10).

We will explore the meaning of self-assessment and why it is important for learning. Pupils' voices provide an account of their experiences of self-assessment and a range of strategies that can effectively develop pupils' skills in self-assessment are discussed.

Figure 4.1 Self-assessment

What is self-assessment?

In a pack produced by the University of Bristol in 1992 for KS2 and beyond, self-assessment was described as a review process that involves the learner in:

• reflecting on past experience
• seeking to remember and understand what took place
• attempting to gain a clearer idea of what has been learned or achieved.

The pack suggested self-assessment would involve pupils in:

• sharing responsibility for the organisation of their work
• keeping records of activities they have undertaken
• making decisions about future actions and targets.

We suggest the underpinning principle of self-assessment is that pupils are more responsible for and involved in their own learning. Therefore self-assessment is closely linked with assessment *for* learning, rather than assessment *of* learning, since assessment is used as a process for improving pupils' learning.

Schools and teachers are already encouraging pupils to undertake this review process: in primary schools ideas of reviewing progress are built into the literacy and numeracy strategies and in secondary schools records of achievement and other review processes are a part of helping pupils prepare for adult life. However, the implications of self-assessment are broader than this, so we consider how effective current self-review processes are and how these ways of working can become more central to teaching and learning.

Self-assessment covers a range of strategies and teaching approaches which can be used in many learning contexts. These will be examined in more detail later, but first it is important to consider how these ideas might affect current classrooms. What compromises might they involve and how might teachers have to change their expectations?

Self-assessment – a new way of thinking?

David Boud (1995), who writes about self-assessment in higher education, makes many points that are relevant to schools, teachers and pupils. He starts by indicating the potentially radical nature of wholeheartedly taking on the issues of self-assessment. 'Self-assessment, while commonly portrayed as a technique to enhance learning, is more transformative, elusive and confronting to conventional teaching than it is commonly expedient to recognise' (Boud, 1995: 1).

This sounds a bit daunting, but teachers have to recognise the power issues involved in classrooms and how their work as teachers is bound up in what they, and pupils, think teachers 'should' be doing. Often this includes making judgements about the merit of work being done, which has usually been seen as the teacher's job, not the pupils'. Taking on a way of working that really values pupils' own ideas about the quality of their work is therefore a possible challenge to the usual order and routine of the classroom. Teachers and pupils may need to find a way to adapt to this challenge.

Who does what?

A starting point is to think about roles within self-assessment: what is the teacher's job and what is the pupil's? David Satterly (1989) discusses this by looking at who has relevant pieces of information. He suggests there are aspects of pupils' work which teachers could expect them to know more about – how hard they worked, what they were trying to achieve, how far they think they have achieved this and how the work relates to their own personal goals. However, pupils are unlikely to know, at least initially, as much as their teacher about the expectations of the curriculum in relation to a piece of work and what criteria will be applied to their work in more formal assessments which will be made. This seems to indicate the need for a partnership in assessment, with each participant contributing different pieces of information that they can use to create a more complete picture.

Perhaps David Satterly's view removes some of the challenge to the teacher's role mentioned above because clearly there are aspects which the teacher will need to lead and control, but by placing the pupils' input centrally within the assessment process he emphasises its contribution to the learning process.

Duncan Harris and Colin Bell (1986) suggest that assessment can be thought of as a continuum from teacher controlled to learner controlled. This continuum features increasing emphasis and responsibility being placed on the learner for their own learning as the methods used move from 'traditional' assessment, through collaborative (teacher and pupil) and peer assessment, to self-assessment. The important idea here is that increasing pupil responsibility may offer a starting point for implementing these ideas in classrooms. Collaborative assessment could be the stepping stone that allows teachers to work with pupils on increasing their responsibility and independence so that they can move towards working with their peers on jointly assessing their progress and then to a more fully fledged ability to understand their own learning and reflect on its quality.

It appears therefore that there are some aspects of assessment, particularly related to effort and motivation, that pupils may already be well placed to judge, but teachers will need to find ways to share their understanding of quality if pupils are to become better at evaluating their own work.

Why is self-assessment important in the learning process?

The role of assessment in supporting learning is, essentially, to identify the gap between current and desired performance and to offer support to the pupil in closing that gap. It is the pupil who needs to make the step forward in their learning, and self-assessment can give them information about their achievements and a better understanding of what is needed to 'close the gap'.

All pupils appear to benefit from learning self-assessment strategies but many high attainers already intuitively self-assess, whereas lower attainers find it more difficult. Teachers can help by working with pupils on developing the skills required. One way to do this is by enhancing the pupil's meta-cognitive skills. Meta-cognition is about understanding and being aware of one's own learning – taking a step outside the learning process to look at it and reflect on it. This is an important part of being an effective learner and can be developed by answering such questions as 'What have I learned?', 'How well have I achieved my targets?', 'How could I do this better in the future?' As people grow older their self-awareness grows and is easier to express, but many teachers have found that by introducing the idea of self-assessment to very young children they can nurture and develop these skills.

Self-assessment is a skill to be learned like any other. Some pupils will initially find self-assessment difficult and will not be motivated by the process. Some may be too hard on themselves, demanding unrealistic achievement and becoming disappointed when they don't achieve their ideal. Others may be complacent and not challenge themselves, being prepared to accept insufficiently high standards.

Nicky Arber, who teaches at Bournville School, Birmingham gives her pupils 'Learning Briefing' sheets (Figure 4.2), a form of advanced organiser, outlining the aims and expected outcomes at the beginning of the lesson. She encourages them to self-assess by asking them to answer 2 or 3 questions about their learning at the end of the lesson. They are encouraged to think about the progress they have made and how they could improve in future. Some of these individual statements are shared around the class. The questions are varied and sufficient time is allowed for the pupils to reflect on and engage with the task. Pupils value this approach because they know what they are doing and why, they are able to identify progress and have some idea about what they need to do next. The information shared provides Nicky with valuable insights into pupils' ways of working and their misconceptions so that she can plan future lessons better.

Ultimately pupils have to do their own learning, but the example above shows how responsibility for developing learning strategies can be shared. The teacher provides the pupils with the support they need and the right stimuli to help them engage, while the pupils take more responsibility for their own learning. Accepting responsibility for learning can be difficult for some pupils, particularly when they feel others are judging their success and controlling their progress. Self-assessment can be a very powerful tool in helping pupils become more aware of the progress they are making towards achieving both short- and long-term targets.

Finally self-assessment is important in that it tends to be *ipsative* (the assessment is compared to the pupil's previous achievement) rather than *normative* (compared with the achievements of other pupils). Many learners have memories of being compared to friends and peers. While this is a natural human characteristic and impossible to eliminate, it is important to recognise the damage that can be done to pupils' confidence and self-esteem. When pupils have a role in assessing their own achievements it allows them to be advocates of their successes and to have these recognised, in their own terms, by their teachers. Pupils know how hard they worked on a task and how they feel about their achievements, and they alone can help teachers understand this. While initially some pupils' judgements may be flawed, the process of testing them against other judgements will quickly result in them becoming better and more consistent.

The links between teaching, self-assessment and motivation

Peter Airasian (1996) makes what should be an obvious link, between teaching and assessment, and points out that in self-assessment the two can be almost indistinguishable. Where does teaching end and assessment begin? 'When students are using the performance criteria to

We are using a range of exercises to . . .

- Help you understand the changes that have occurred in the manufacturing industries of France.
- Examine the characteristics and reasons for the development of Technopoles.

These are our learning goals . . .

By the end of the lesson you MUST have done the following:
- Defined old and new industries.

- Matched the beginnings and endings of a range of statements.

- Completed an interview with a French businessman.

- Created a newspaper article which looks at the manufacturing industry of France.

By the end of the lesson you SHOULD have used the following skills:
- Rearranged information to create statements.

- Investigated the factors affecting manufacturing change in France.

- Consolidated ideas by completing the newspaper front page.

- Shared information and understanding with others.

- Interpreted a range of text.

- Reflected upon what you know, understand and can do.

As part of your homework you COULD:
- Compare and contrast the changes which have occurred in the manufacturing industry and farming.

Figure 4.2 Learning briefing sheet

review their own or another pupil's writing, they are neither solely assessing nor solely learning, they are using assessment as a means of learning' (Airasian, 1996: 161). Teaching, learning and assessment are always closely linked, but in using self-assessment strategies a teacher further blurs the dividing line, as a pupil's learning activities will involve aspects of assessment of those activities.

Linking teaching, learning and self-assessment can be an important motivator, as discussed in Chapter 3. Motivated pupils tend to learn better and behave better. Pupils often see assessment as a threatening event. The merging of teaching and self-assessment can put it back into its true place as a supportive and motivating part of the learning process that can help them with the many external assessment events in their school lives.

In Chapter 1 we discussed the emotional impact of assessment. Self-assessment is particularly emotionally challenging and pupils will need their teachers' support and guidance if they are to use self-assessment for effective learning. Most people when thinking back to their own experiences of assessing themselves remember uncomfortable experiences as well as motivating and empowering ones.

Comments or grades about effort are very widely used in schools but can be unhelpful to pupils. It is worth considering how difficult it is to accurately reward effort when judging outcomes. A task that is easy for one child may be very challenging for another and a teacher will have difficulty assessing these differences. What could be more demotivating for a pupil than to be constantly told 'try harder' when they know they are already trying hard? Self-assessment allows pupils to more meaning-fully share information with their teachers so that they feel they have a role in the decision making about their learning.

What is currently happening in schools?

So far in this chapter we have looked at the perceived benefits of self-assessment as outlined by some of its advocates. In the next section we consider two self-assessment strategies used by schools over the last 15 years and look at pupils' experience of self-assessment.

Two examples of self-assessment occurring in schools

In the early days of National Curriculum implementation many schools began to use some self-assessment strategies, particularly to help them assess the 'process' areas of the curriculum. Pupils became used to self-assessment pro-formas that asked them to rate their performance in a given task against criteria derived from the process attainment targets of the National Curriculum. Some schools found these useful, although there was a tendency for their completion to become rather routine and for pupils to lack real understanding of what was being asked.

Similarly over the last 15 years, records of achievement have given pupils an opportunity to reflect on their own learning and to record their views of their achievements. The broader view of achievement which these records allow is an important feature as it supports motivation through recognition of otherwise possibly unvalued achievements of pupils.

Both these self-assessment strategies are a step towards pupils understanding their own progress and being able to see how to move their learning forward. They also provide an important mechanism for the learners' first steps towards lifelong learning to be recorded. If school life is the first experience in a continuing programme of learning, the pupil's responsibility for contributing to the record of achievement is an important recognition of their role. However, like any learning strategy they have to be valued by the learner, the school and society, thereby gaining the social currency discussed in Chapter 2. Unfortunately there is evidence that because they are time-consuming and often organised in rather mechanistic ways, their value in contributing to developing broader self-assessment skills is reduced.

The pupils' perspective

The researchers in the LEARN project (Weeden and Winter, 1999) discussed with pupils whether they used self-assessment strategies. Disappointingly there was little evidence of self-assessment being used as a strategy to support learning, and where pupils reported having used self-assessment the examples they gave suggested that it involved them in little more than a mechanical marking process:

> Sometimes in the whole class – he does it on the board and we mark our own. (Y6)

> Once in maths I ticked my own work. It's not good to mark your own work because you don't know if it's right or wrong. (Y3)

Three main themes emerged from the research:

- Pupils need convincing that they have a role in assessment of their work.
- Some pupils can and do self-assess.
- Pupils feel more confident when they understand what they have to do and how the outcomes will be assessed.

Assessment is the teacher's job!

Some pupils had strong views about the teacher's 'job' and their own role:

> In English we have a partner and you swap books and you assess them and the teacher takes them in. I don't like that really. It's better if the teacher does it. (Y9)

> We sometimes assess our own work in Science – it's a waste of time. (GCSE)

This suggests that many pupils are overdependent on teachers for aspects of their learning. Pupils believed the teacher should be telling them if they had done well or not, apparently because they were unclear about the criteria for judging their work. However, there were examples of peer marking that were more positive for pupils because they helped them engage with aspects of quality:

> Sometimes we swap books with our neighbours and see what we've got wrong. If we've got any spelling mistakes they underline it and we check it again. Then I've got two opinions on it. (Y9)

There were rare mentions of some peer and self-assessment, particularly in English:

> Sometimes we think about how we could have done better and how we could have improved it. Usually happens mostly in English and written subjects – not maths. (Y9)

> Just before Christmas we gave each lesson the number we thought and the teacher did the same. Most of the grades I gave were the same as the teacher. (GCSE)

There were a few examples of teachers using strategies to help pupils assess their own work:

> In geography we had an essay and he said try to pick out the mistakes and give it a mark out of 20. It was good to see what kind of mistakes we make. (GCSE)

> If it said to get level 7 do extension work, it would make you go and do the extension work. It saves time – you feel more independent on yourself. (GCSE)

These examples were mostly given by older pupils, although some younger pupils may not have recognised the experiences they were having as ones where self-assessment was involved.

Figure 4.3 'We think we know where we went wrong!'

the pupil to comment on how well they think they have achieved them. They can be combined with a comment from the teacher in response. Two important factors in making this method successful are that it should not become a meaningless routine and that the outcomes of the assessment should be used in future work – it needs to lead the pupils' learning forward.

Using examples of assessed work

Mary James (1998) suggests using examples of assessed work because they help pupils understand what criteria really mean in practice. Criteria when written can often be quite general but looking at specific examples can help pupils see how to improve their own work. Pupils can get a clearer understanding of how criteria are used by looking at the assessment of the sample work and identifying what was valued, what was not, what was an important aspect of the work and what was less important. This exercise should give pupils (and teachers) an opportunity not just to look at relatively simple criteria such as spelling and punctuation but also to consider more complex and subjective criteria such as the difference between description and explanation, or how to analyse and synthesise evidence.

Understanding purpose

There are many ways of helping pupils understand what is required in their work, some of which have been discussed before. This understanding is essential if self-assessment is to develop their learning more effectively. Three examples of ways that pupils can develop better understanding of the purpose of their learning are:

- paired or group discussion of targets for a piece of work
- working with a partner to look at part of a textbook or resource and identifying its main aims
- setting their own tasks (and tests!), identifying the purpose and producing criteria for assessment.

Discussion

The content and level of the interaction between teacher and pupils, and between pupils, is crucial to learning, and building discussion into learning activities is a vital way of raising the quality of both. Pupils can learn through discussion of their work with their peers and through 'real' discussion of it with their teachers. Much 'discussion' in classrooms can, through pressure, really be nothing more than the teacher telling (again). If discussion can develop so that pupils are heard and the teacher's response is designed to stimulate the pupils' thinking, learning is more likely to be improved.

Why is this part of self-assessment? Because when pupils talk about their work they are forced to structure it in their minds and thus learn more about what they know and what they are still unsure of. This is why it is the pupils' talking which is important and the teacher's response needs to be appropriate.

Interviews

This takes the idea of discussion of work a little further. Pupils can be asked to review their progress on a topic in an interview and then listen to a tape of the interview to consider how well the learning identified matches the learning criteria. This encourages pupils to step back from their immediate reactions and to reflect on them.

Journals

Pupils can be asked to keep learning journals in which they reflect on their progress. To be successful this must be kept alive and not allowed to become a repetitive activity. Pupils can quickly run out of things to write and then revert to stock stereotyped responses if they are not encouraged to link their writing closely with the desired learning outcomes. Pupils can write perceptively on what they have learned, providing valuable assessment information for teachers.

Portfolios

This is a method of evidence collection that has waxed and waned in popularity over the years since the introduction of the National

Curriculum. For self-assessment, its value is in offering pupils the opportunity to make decisions about the relative merits of pieces of work they have done and to develop a collection of pieces that they feel best reflects their achievement. This is not about coverage of attainment targets or levels, although that may form part of the way selections are made, but about pupils reflecting on their achievements and being enabled to take pleasure and pride in them.

The strategies outlined above are merely starting points and should be seen as generic strategies that can be adapted for different contexts. We have argued earlier in the book that effective learning is strongly linked to self-esteem and motivation; self-assessment strategies can play a major role in sustaining both these facilitators of learning. If teachers can build self-assessment into their own preferred ways of working they will be able to broaden the range of experiences for their pupils.

Recording

The results of assessments are recorded for a range of purposes. Teachers may want to report to parents or others on pupils' progress or to use assessment records for evaluation of the effectiveness of their teaching. There is no reason why pupils' own self-assessments should not play a major part in meeting both these needs. If teachers have a system of self-assessment in pupils' books, a special folder or a diary these can be used to support other records of pupils' achievements and assessments. Pupils' written comments can be collected and brief notes of assessment discussions used as part of the evaluation of teaching. In short, all the same information can be gathered and recorded from self-assessments as from other forms of assessment.

Peer assessment

This has been included as a separate section because there are some aspects of peer assessment that are slightly different from self-assessment. One advantage of peer assessment is that it contributes to pupils' personal and social development. Individual pupils learn how to communicate with their peers in non-judgmental ways. They soon find that if they want constructive feedback they have to be sensitive about the kind of feedback they give others. The shared understanding of learning can help pupils develop through seeing other ways of looking at a problem. What is valued is no longer simply 'what the teacher says' but expands to include understanding someone else's viewpoint.

If pupils are working with a set of criteria that they have discussed and developed together they have a clearer understanding of what is expected. The process of looking at each other's work and judging it against those criteria allows them to think about the relative merits of their own performance. It allows them to identify strengths and weaknesses in their work and if they are then required to revise their work they can improve it because they understand it better. This is a more constructive form of comparison between pupils than merely telling them their relative performance within the group, without offering any insight into how to improve their work.

Time issues

With all the demands made on time in schools today, have teachers really got time to spend doing some of the activities suggested in this chapter? We argue that if learning can become more effective, time can be saved not lost, but we also recognise that this is not a short-term process. Teachers have all experienced working with a new class or group and finding that it takes time for them to 'do things their way'. Pupils can and do become expert at learning what different teachers expect of them.

The introduction and use of self-assessment is one more way in which pupils need to get to know what is expected of them and one more set of 'classroom rules' that they need to understand. By making some clear changes to classroom routines teachers can make these new expectations clear. Posters on the wall with some key self-assessment questions are an excellent starting point:

- What have I learned?
- What am I most pleased with about my work?
- What did I find difficult?
- How can I try to improve this?

These review questions can be used at regular intervals to remind pupils about areas they should be thinking about to help them focus on their learning.

There are other ways of helping pupils become more independent in their work. Making resources available to them rather than requiring them to be dependent on the teacher for what they want is one key method used in primary classrooms. All classrooms can achieve this to some extent, and the pupils themselves are a valuable resource in this respect. If pupils are given responsibility for aspects of classroom organisation and management, this will rub off on their attitude to their work. Taking responsibility can improve motivation and behaviour, can give pupils a real feeling for their role in the learning process and reduces the feeling that they are there merely to 'receive' passively.

Another aspect of managing pupils' and teachers' time is linked to expectations about communication. Do teachers run round classrooms, at the mercy of a sea of hands? Or do pupils learn to be more self-reliant in their work, to ask themselves and their neighbours and other resources for help before switching off, putting up their hands and waiting? If classrooms can be organised so that pupils are more self-reliant, time can be made for different kinds of interactions between teacher and pupils and between pupils themselves in which self-assessment activity can take place. This highlights the fact that self-assessment has wide implications for the teaching and learning process and may have important impacts on teaching style and classroom management.

Implementation problems

One of the difficulties teachers face in making self-assessment a meaningful part of pupils' learning is helping pupils to move from a purely descriptive approach to one which really shows understanding of the learning process and awareness of how their understanding has grown. Pupils' early responses on being asked to evaluate their work are usually simplistic and superficial: 'I liked this' or 'I think I did this quite well'. It takes time to help them move beyond this kind of answer to answers which really help them decide what they need to work on and how to go about this. Teachers' questions need to focus on the intended learning outcomes and to indicate to pupils what sort of answers are wanted. Pupils may need to hear some suggested answers to give them an idea of how to answer such questions. They can then think about how their answers would differ from what the teacher is suggesting and thus understand more about what they have learned.

As suggested above, discussion between pupils can be an effective way for them to think about their own learning. They will hear from their peers how they tackled a task and can think about what they have achieved through sharing the language used by their peers. This can help to overcome some of the problems associated with writing which younger or lower-attaining pupils may find get in the way. Pupils may be able to express themselves orally in a much deeper way than they can in writing – after all, it is not always the pupils' writing skills that we want them to assess. The format can get in the way of the intention.

One frequent difficulty with self-assessment, when it is not really a meaningful part of learning, is that it can become repetitive and routine: 'Oh, here we go again, it's the self-assessment sheet that we do at the end of every piece of work'. Pupils need to get something out of the process for it to be valued by them. If they see self-assessment as something they are doing for the teacher, not for themselves, then it will not have any impact on how they think of themselves as learners. Keep it varied and lively – use different methods, different groupings, different formats and appropriate ways of addressing different kinds of topic. And above all, help pupils see the impact of the self-assessment activity on future work – refer to their statements about their learning in your feedback to them on subsequent pieces of work: 'Well done, you said last time that you were pleased with your use of adjectives, this time you have also varied your sentence structure to make your story more lively'.

Finally expect pupils to challenge you! If pupils are encouraged to take more responsibility for their own learning then they are also likely to be more demanding. They may report that an activity was boring or too hard – be ready to listen, reflect on and respond to this kind of assessment too.

Conclusion

In this chapter we have provided evidence that self-assessment has the potential to raise performance. We have also suggested that using self-assessment has consequences for ways of working and relationships in the classroom, and requires pupils to take more responsibility for their own learning. Even young children can engage in self-assessment if it is presented in the right way. The benefits include greater self-esteem and motivation, particularly for lower attainers, who will need the greatest assistance with developing self-assessment skills. The challenge for teachers is to find strategies that they feel comfortable with and that work in their context. We have outlined a number of strategies, and hope that you will feel able to try some of them in your classroom. A good starting point is to build review times into the end of the lesson, but to vary the strategies used so that they don't become repetitive.

ACTIVITIES

1   What are your own experiences of self-assessment?

What have your experiences of self-assessment been? Think through learning situations you have been in (school, higher education, learning to drive, learning to cook, personal interests . . .).

In which of these situations have you made your own assessments of your progress and achievements?

Have these assessments been a recognised part of your achievement profile or have they been private and used only by you?

What was the value of the assessments you made? How did they affect your progress? How did you feel about the recognition (or lack of it) which they received?

2   Sharing learning intentions and reviewing progress

Plan one lesson so that you clearly share the purpose and outcomes of the lesson with the class. At the end of the lesson ask them some review questions, get them to record them and then have a group discussion.

How successful were you and what have you learnt about the group and individuals?

3   Trying self-assessment!

Plan to incorporate self-assessment into a programme of teaching. If you can, find a colleague to discuss the ideas with and to observe some of the work and evaluate it with you. This will allow you an outsider's view of what is happening as well as your own.

What outcomes do you hope to achieve?

Review the success of your strategies, remembering that things don't all work out overnight. What is worth developing further? What are the strengths which you have to build on? What amendments do you feel would help improve the outcomes?

4   How is self-assessment used in your school?

Talk to a small number of pupils whom you teach about self-assessment. Do they understand the term? Do they have experiences of it in their own learning? Do other teachers they have worked with use it? How do they feel about it?

Talk to other teachers in your school. Do they use self-assessment? What do they mean by the term if they do use it? What do they feel are the benefits to their teaching and their pupils' learning? Discuss your shared understanding of self-assessment. Do you mean the same thing when you use the term?

5 How can marking and feedback help pupils learn?

> Regular marking should inform the teacher of pupils' progress, stimulate dialogue about the work and encourage pupils to improve. However these powerful potential benefits of marking are only sometimes realised. The frequency and quality of marking vary unacceptably, within and across departments and between schools.
>
> (OFSTED, 1998: 92)

We have argued throughout this book that assessment cannot be separated from the teaching and learning process. In this chapter we suggest that effective marking and feedback that informs and 'feeds forward' into future work must be vital elements of teaching if we want to improve learning and raise standards for all pupils.

Figure 5.1 Effective questioning promotes learning

We start the chapter by identifying some principles of marking and feedback. These are then given a different perspective by considering the pupils' view of these two areas. Finally we consider how teachers can use both marking and feedback more effectively.

Some principles of marking and feedback

The bad old days?

One of us remembers marking (many years ago) at the beginning of his career.

My frustration when assessing pupils' learning of a topic was that I wasn't sure how to assess what had been learnt. The pupils did a series of activities and had lots of work in their books, but surely I needed to check what they'd learnt over the last few weeks. Unfortunately although we had covered the content of the topic, I didn't always have a clear idea about what I wanted them to have learnt and how I could find out.

If I used a test it tended to focus on random 'bits' of knowledge from the topic and get a mark out of 10 or 20. If I used a task I tended to mark generic skills such as spelling, punctuation, grammar and map skills, develop an impression of how good the geography was and record this as a grade in my book. If I marked work in their books much of it was just 'tick and flick' to make sure they had done the work set. With all these assessments, any misunderstandings were only picked up by chance, because I wasn't clear about what I wanted to assess – I wasn't using the assessment to effectively diagnose learning difficulties.

Another problem then occurred. Once I'd got this information what should I do with it and what did it mean? Tests gave me a mark but how could I use the information? Tasks took time to mark so that by the time the pupils got their work back we had usually moved onto another topic and any comments I gave to individual pupils weren't followed up because they weren't relevant to the current topic.

What I did have however was a set of marks in my mark book that I could use at parents evenings to make comments about pupils. However most of the time my comments were based more upon information stored in my head and were often very bland or focused on behaviour and attitude more than understanding of the subject. Comments such as 'Works hard and is always keen to learn' or 'More attention in class and less chat to others is needed. Is capable of doing much better' were typical.

This account, by highlighting the tensions and confusions that this beginning teacher faced when marking work, is a good starting point for examining some principles of marking and feedback.

Marking is only one way of collecting assessment information but it plays an important part in most teachers' lives, while giving and receiving marks is one of the commonest ways of communication between teacher and pupils. We will explore the principles of marking and feedback by discussing a series of important questions.

What are pupils expected to learn?

The beginning teacher above is describing a common phenomenon, their lack of clarity about learning objectives and how to identify and communicate the concepts of their subject at an appropriate level for the pupils. As a result their marking may be unfocused. Unfortunately this phenomenon is not restricted to beginning teachers, although the National Curriculum has helped teachers by giving assessment criteria within the level descriptions.

How can outcomes be assessed?

The important point here is that any assessment has to be 'fit for purpose'. For example, practical skills can't be assessed appropriately through a written theoretical test and short factual answers in a test may not assess thinking skills. The key therefore is to devise assessments that are appropriate and find ways to 'mark' them successfully. Finally it should be remembered that any assessment only gives a partial view of the learner's knowledge, skill and understanding so if we want a more complete picture it will be necessary to 'mark' outcomes in a variety of different situations thus gaining a fuller understanding of a pupil's achievements.

What should be marked?

This might seem clear. Surely teachers should mark everything pupils do so that they know how learning is progressing? But it isn't as simple as that. Does this imply that every spelling should be corrected, every arithmetic error marked wrong and so on? In fact teachers who use marking to focus on pupil learning make more subtle decisions, based on what they feel will lead to the best learning outcomes. For example, if such a teacher sees a string of arithmetical errors based on the same misconception, they will plan to address that misconception rather than simply present the pupil with a string of crosses.

How can marking be prioritised and rationalised?

A related issue is that if every piece of work done or task undertaken has to be marked it can be far too time-consuming and can lead to a 'flick and tick' approach that merely indicates work has been completed. Teachers who are aware of this focus their marking on significant pieces of work that provide information about the pupils' current understanding or misconceptions. To do this successfully they must be clear about their intended learning outcomes and know the assessment criteria they plan to use so that they can target their feedback.

Teachers may choose to include 'trick' questions that they think will help identify misconceptions and allow them to check whether pupils have a deep or surface understanding of the topic. For example, a primary teacher attempting to identify pupils' misconceptions about perspective on maps might ask the pupils to draw a map of their school, making sure they mark on some significant buildings. An analysis of the way they draw the buildings can allow the teacher to make a tentative judgement about their understanding of perspective.

The teacher is looking to see whether the pupils draw the buildings from above as a 'bird's eye view' or from the side. By questioning the pupils after they have completed the task the teacher can decide if they

Map of our school (Year 3)

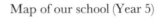

Map of our school (Year 5)

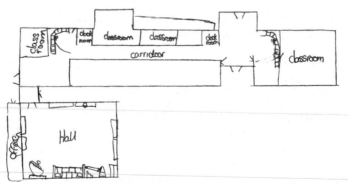

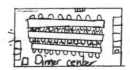

Figure 5.2 Maps of a school

know about the map convention of drawing buildings as if viewed from above, if they are using a side view of a house because that's the view they normally see or using it as a 'symbolic' representation of a house. The results will guide the teacher's planning about future teaching and learning activities for these pupils.

Sometimes teachers might want to involve pupils more actively in making decisions about their own learning, as outlined in Chapter 4. To do this they might involve the pupils in 'self-assessment', marking their own or peers' work and maybe even deciding on criteria for judgements. This has the benefit of being another way of rationalising marking. It is not merely a way of reducing the teacher's work, but can lead to new and important pupil learning outcomes, which may not happen if they merely 'passively' respond to external marking of their work.

When is the marking carried out?

The beginning teacher's account suggests that the assessments used were 'bolted on' to the rest of the work, rather than integral activities. The marking was used to collect summative information, giving an indication of the learning at that time, and little attempt was made to use it formatively. If marking is to be formative it has to be planned for, be part of the ongoing work, and be used to inform future work. As a result 'marking' for formative purposes will take place at a variety of times and be integral to the teaching and learning process.

How quickly should feedback occur?

Pupils (and teachers) tend to forget work quickly. They move on to new priorities so, to have significant impact, feedback should occur quickly. This has important implications for teachers' marking and implies careful planning.

It may be that if a 'test' or 'task' is being used formatively it needs to be marked immediately, by the pupils, so that it is an integral part of the teaching and learning process. In this case the teacher is less concerned about the reliability of the marks and more about the impact of the test on motivation and learning.

How is achievement recorded?

Most secondary teachers keep records of outcomes in mark books, but marks alone may not give sufficient information about knowledge, understanding and skills for meaningful comments to be made about pupils. Primary teachers are perhaps more familiar with other forms of record keeping, such as day books, notes of significant events, portfolios or mark books that record a wide range of data. This issue of recording is returned to in Chapter 6.

To summarise, we suggest that some *principles for marking and feedback* are:

- Marking should be linked to clear learning objectives.
- Assessments should be 'fit for purpose' and have appropriate mark schemes.
- Marking should help identify pupil misconceptions.
- Marking should be focused and prioritised.
- Marking needs to be planned for and be integral to teaching and learning.
- Marking and feedback should take place quickly so that pupils remember the context.
- Recording may need to take a variety of forms that are manageable but informative.

What do pupils feel about the feedback they receive?

In this section we look at feedback from the pupils' perspective to gain an insight into what they feel does and doesn't help their learning. A large number of pupils were asked about the feedback they received on their work and how they felt about it. They also showed the researchers some of their work and discussed what they understood by the feedback on it (Weeden and Winter, 1999).

Types of feedback

As you might expect, there was a very wide range of feedback used by teachers, with grades, ticks and crosses, smiley faces, written and oral comments being the most common. All of these methods provoked emotional responses from children:

If there's a star in pen that Miss wrote, then you have to write it three times – that's the boringest part. (Y3)

If it's a tick I'm quite happy because it means its good work, but if it's 2 sentences at the bottom it means it's quite bad. (Y6)

Some teachers put things you could work on to make it better. I like that cos you can work on it more. (Y9)

Pupils recognised the importance of feedback in helping them learn, although they didn't always like the comments they received. They wanted feedback to be directed towards improving their work and they liked having verbal feedback because they felt they learnt more effectively.

What the teacher says is most important because it's one on one so they can tell you what they really think. (Y9)

They usually say how well you researched and how you didn't put in enough effort. They give you positive feedback as well. They give you tips on how you could improve. (Y9)

If we don't understand things they get explained to us. If it's just written you can't ask a question directly. If you talk you can say how can I improve it. (Y10)

Comments make you think about the other things you've got to put in next time to get a better grade – it's good to know what you've done wrong. (Y10)

If they correct spelling I can sort it out. If they left them I wouldn't know how to spell the word. (Y10)

Do pupils understand the grades they receive?

But what about the grades often used on pupils' work in secondary schools? There was a lot of confusion amongst pupils about what they meant. For example, if a grading system for achievement used numbers 1 to 5, some pupils did not know which was better, 1 or 5. In a letter/ number pair for achievement and effort, some were confused about which was which. And within schools if teachers used varying systems pupils were even more likely to be confused. This poses a major problem for teachers and schools – if some pupils don't understand the grades they receive, can they really be that useful?

Another problem with grades is that they don't offer any advice on how to improve. For instance, if pupils get a C this doesn't tell them how they could have got a B.

How do pupils react to written comments?

The other main type of written feedback on work is comments on what pupils have done. Pupils again have strong emotional reactions to these and they don't necessarily make much use of them. Here are a few comments from pupils that reflect the range of reactions found:

> Good doesn't help much – he's just saying that it's not really very good. I'd like it if he just told the truth. (Y3)

> 'Not very good work' doesn't help me to know how to do it better. (Y3)

> Good or excellent gives you confidence in what you're doing. (Y6)

> If they give you tips on how you could improve and say what you did well it's a lot nicer. It boosts your confidence more. (Y9)

> Sometimes he says it could be better but if I think I've done it well I just forget about it. (Y9)

> She says to spend more time on it – that's about it actually. (Y9)

> Once she said, 'You're not very good at spelling'. I don't really want to hear that because I already know that. (Y10)

> *'Do you read what the teacher writes?'* 'No, I just keep on writing.' (Y10)

> Comments are useful because you get to know how to improve. Like it says there – 'one too many rhetorical questions'. (A level)

To summarise, the main points that arise from the pupils' experiences are:

- Pupils receive feedback in a variety of forms.
- Pupils like verbal feedback because they feel they learn more.
- Grading systems often confuse pupils.

- Feedback strongly affects pupils' self-esteem and motivation.
- Some pupils respond positively to feedback that gives guidance on how to improve their work.

How can marking and feedback be used to improve learning?

The rest of this chapter considers how marking and feedback might be used to improve learning. Paul Black and Dylan Wiliam (1998a), as reported in Chapter 2, suggest that feedback is one of the key factors in promoting learning. Why then is much current feedback either unhelpful or ignored by pupils and why is marking seen by many teachers as a chore?

How can marking help learning?

As we discussed earlier in the chapter, marking can be a complex process. When faced with a set of books, teachers have to ask themselves, how can I mark this work, what am I looking for? The beginning teacher often isn't sure whether to focus on the quality of the content, the language or the presentation, while the experienced teacher may trust in their intuition and past experience (see Curtis, Weeden and Winter, 2000). Too often the result is that marking merely focuses on correcting spellings, judging presentation and giving an overall impression mark based on an imprecise idea of a 'perfect' answer.

How can marking be more focused so that it can be used formatively to help pupils learn? One way is to have a mark scheme that clearly identifies expected outcomes, particularly if more than one teacher is using the assessment. There are two common forms of mark scheme, point-credit and level of response, both of which can be used either formatively or summatively.

Example 1: A test with a *point-credit mark scheme*
A test has a series of questions with a reasonably limited range of possible answers. Some questions require factual recall, some allow

---

pupils to show understanding, some require them to use skills and some may require analysis and explanation. Marks are awarded for specific responses. This type of mark scheme, where marks are awarded for each correct point up to a pre-defined limit, is known as a point-credit mark scheme.

David Lambert and David Lines (2000) argue that this type of assessment is widely used because it copies the summative assessments that are so prevalent within the English education system and teachers feel that this type of assessment gives them an objective view of pupil performance. It is however worth asking how *valid* this type of test is in showing what pupils know, understand and can do, because the type of questions that can be asked and therefore the knowledge or skills tested are limited.

A further issue to consider with point-credit mark schemes is whether different markers will use them in the same way. This is an issue for all mark schemes where more than one person uses them but many people think because this type of mark scheme is 'objective' in nature it will be *reliable* when used by different markers. In fact, experience shows that unless the mark scheme is very detailed and well written different markers are likely to interpret it in a variety of ways so a pupil's score might vary depending on the marker. When these types of mark scheme are used in external examinations such as GCSE, chief examiners have to go through each question in detail with all markers to ensure that they interpret the mark scheme consistently. This is important to remember if results are used summatively, for instance to place pupils into sets.

Computer-based testing is being marketed as a diagnostic tool that will help identify weaknesses that can be followed up by the teacher. For example, by using a computer-based test a teacher was able to identify two pupils who didn't understand the relationship of adjacent, opposite and hypotenuse in a right angled triangle. He might not have picked this up through his normal teaching and assessment unless he had specifically targeted this problem.

> The teachers and the pupils look forward to the tests so it's full steam ahead! It gives us results and information we couldn't get before and helps us to focus our teaching on areas of weakness.

Aimed primarily at the National Curriculum, it helps us to measure where we really are so that we can meet the targets.

(GOAL on-line assessment system publicity brochure, 2001)

The point to emphasise here is that point-credit marking can provide teachers with a lot of valuable formative information, if they can find ways of accessing it. The best of these types of assessments are planned to be part of the teaching programme and constructed to include questions that test known areas of weakness or likely misconceptions. Since the test is integral to the teaching and learning process, the information gathered feeds forward into future work.

Example 2: A task with a *level of response mark scheme*

A class of year 4 pupils are asked to write about a topic they've been studying. The mark scheme for this writing has three levels and uses criteria such as knowledge, analysis and communication skills. This is known as a level of response mark scheme and the work is assessed more holistically by looking for the best fit against the statements in the mark scheme. This type of mark scheme is often derived from National Curriculum level descriptions or is used for essay style questions in external examinations such as GCSE or A-level.

Making judgements against level of response criteria emphasises the 'art' of educational assessment. There are similar issues of reliability in different teachers applying this type of mark scheme so moderation is required to ensure that two or more people marking the same piece of work will make broadly similar judgements. However, experience shows that this can be achieved fairly quickly.

A level of response mark scheme is helpful for formative assessment where the differences between the levels are reasonably clear. This helps teachers identify how pupils can progress from one level to the next. Pupils can then be given a comment such as,

Your work describes one fact about the topic; to make it a better answer you need to describe at least two more and explain how each one might cause problems for people.

The most effective feedback makes these comments into targets that are focused and achievable.

To use either type of mark scheme formatively, teachers have to analyse each answer carefully to see where individuals or groups of pupils have made mistakes, so that they can identify aspects that are causing problems. This can be time-consuming, but there is help with externally set examinations. For the 2000 National Curriculum assessments in English, mathematics and science there are reports (QCA, 2001a and b) that have done much of this analysis and identified strengths and weaknesses in children's performance. At GCSE and A level yearly examiners' reports and mark schemes can provide guidance about performance on past papers. When these papers are set as mock exams teachers can discuss the information in these reports with pupils to help them understand common misconceptions and problems.

Sharing mark schemes with pupils

The most effective learning occurs where pupils understand not just *what* they have to do, but *why* they have to do it and *how it will be judged*.

To achieve this assessment criteria written for teachers will need to be rewritten for pupils. This gives both the assessor and the pupil a clearer idea of the expectations for the task. However, being precise is not possible or desirable for all tasks where being so explicit may limit the quality of the answer. In these cases it is possible to tell pupils the general framework for their work, thus providing an advanced organiser.

For example:

> *You have to write an episode for a TV soap . . . You will be marked on how you structure your story lines – there must be at least two ongoing stories woven together and you must end with an unfinished dramatic scene. You will not be marked on your spelling, punctuation and grammar because we're looking at the quality of your story lines, how you weave them together and whether you've kept the reader interested so that they want to find out what happens next.*

How can teachers make their marking SMART?

The examples given above emphasise again the importance of being clear about the value and place of assessment within the teaching and learning process. If marking is to be SMART teachers should:

- plan to identify their assessment objectives clearly *before* the work is set
- write assessment criteria in pupil language
- share assessment objectives with the pupils
- make assessment an integral part of teaching and learning
- be focused about what they mark in detail
- use 'tick and flick' only for checking completion of routine work
- use marking to identify pupil misconceptions
- create time for providing constructive feedback
- use information gathered to inform the planning and teaching of future work.

Why is feedback important?

Pupils can react to feedback in both positive and negative ways. It is important to remember that giving and receiving feedback is a complex process that is strongly influenced by a number of factors including cues, task, situation and personality.

Kluger and DeNisi in 1996 reviewed the research about feedback and found that feedback can be both beneficial and harmful to future performance. They suggested that there are broadly four types of action by pupils in response to feedback.

- They attempt to reach the standard. This happens when the goal is clear, the pupil's commitment is high and they believe they can succeed (mastery performance).
- They abandon the standard completely. Their belief in their success is low (learned helplessness).
- They change the standard. They may lower the standard to make the goal easier or they can raise the standard if the feedback suggests the gap is small.
- They deny that a standard gap exists.

The best feedback effects occur therefore when the gap between desired and achieved performance is clearly identified and the feedback doesn't feed into existing self-perceptions; for example, pupils low in self-esteem may be particularly anxious to avoid negative feedback. This is a highly complex area that requires more research to understand better the relationship between factors such as gender, social class and race, self-perception and motivation. What is clear is that school, classroom, family and community cultures can play an important part in pupils' ability to understand and act on feedback.

How can feedback help learning?

Giving effective feedback is one of the most important ways in which a teacher can focus on the specific needs of each pupil. Ideally teachers will be aware of the effect that the feedback they give has on their pupils and recognise that tasks and pupils' responses to them vary, as do their learning styles, personalities and backgrounds.

Chapter 3 highlighted that the most effective feedback encourages pupils to focus on the quality of the task rather than the quality of the performance. Feedback such as

> *Your introduction and beginning of the story are exciting and get the reader interested but the story line then becomes too obvious. Think about how you could keep the suspense going – keep your reader guessing until the end about what's going to happen.*

is better than

> *Good introduction but as always your ending is weak. You must try to work harder at developing an interesting story line.*

This illustrates how cues in the feedback message may impact on pupils' self-esteem, causing them to divert their attention away from the task. Since it can be difficult for pupils to disentangle the task from the performance, teachers might consider these questions:

- Have they understood what the pupil was trying to communicate?
- Does the feedback support learning by commenting on the quality of the task?
- How do pupils feel about the feedback they get?

There is plenty of room for misunderstandings between pupils and teacher, both in pupils' work and in teachers' responses to it, so creating a climate of good communication in classrooms is important when providing feedback that will help pupils move forward in their learning.

Closing the gap

Many researchers have focused on the quality of feedback and its effectiveness in helping learners. One interesting finding, reported by Paul Black and Dylan Wiliam (1998a: 9), is that feedback focused on identifying specific errors and poor use of strategies, which then gave learners direct advice on how to improve, was far more effective than marking which simply identified 'right' and 'wrong' responses. This should be obvious, but it is useful to be reminded that work put into providing full and carefully focused feedback can help learning. This finding highlights the idea that feedback is an opportunity to complete the circle in the learning process. It helps pupils understand how to 'close the gap' between their present performance and the desired learning outcomes.

Some common issues associated with feedback

We will now explore four issues, arising from the research, that teachers and schools should consider if they are serious about raising standards. However, a note of caution: these issues are complex and responses will depend on the school context, teacher beliefs and attitudes and pupil dispositions.

The four issues are:

- Does giving grades or comments enhance pupil performance?
- How does feedback affect motivation?
- How do pupils respond to feedback?
- How can teacher record keeping be linked to feedback?

Does giving grades or comments enhance pupil performance?

An important issue facing all schools is the grading of pupils' work. Black and Wiliam (1998b: 49) highlighted this issue by giving an example of research that showed how the form of feedback given might affect future performance.

A group of students were divided into four and were either given feedback in the form of comments, grades or praise, or were given no feedback at all. Those in the first group, given comments only, scored considerably higher on later tests than those in any other group. The students given praise thought they were performing well but in fact were performing no better than students given grades or no feedback.

This research questions the value of grades and challenges the impact of one of the commonest methods of giving feedback. Grading is done in many ways: common forms are marks out of 10, National Curriculum levels, or letters and/or numbers for effort and attainment. Pupils are often confused about the meaning of grades, as previously discussed on pp. 102–3.

Figure 5.3 Grades don't help pupils understand how to improve their performance

How does feedback affect motivation?

Feedback can have important motivational effects, both positive and negative. Comments and other feedback can influence how pupils feel about themselves as learners, which in turn affects their future learning.

Pupils whose aims are defined in terms of mastery-oriented goals (see Chapter 3), and who want to 'master' some learning, have been shown to learn more effectively than those whose aims relate to 'performance', for example, merely wanting to get good grades. If feedback is linked too strongly to performance goals, for instance 'that work was worth a level 3/4/5', pupils will not be encouraged to learn as effectively. If however feedback is focused on recognising the mastery they are achieving, for example, 'You clearly describe some of the causes of the French Revolution and how it affected different people's lives', learning is more likely to happen.

How do pupils respond to feedback?

Feedback can have a strong impact on pupils' emotions, self-esteem and motivation. Personal individual feedback can be very powerful, with pupils being strongly affected by the way their teachers respond to them. Teachers may unintentionally fail to give pupils the attention they think their work deserves or it may be treated with less attention and care because of other pressures.

Shared communal activities that go on in classrooms can lead to feedback being given publicly and spontaneously. How does the teacher respond when a pupil answers an oral question with an incorrect answer? The answer to this question will depend on the circumstances and the nature of the question but the feedback given in these inter-active situations is just as important as the more considered comments written in pupils' more private books. Teachers need to think quickly, both about their assessment of the pupil's understanding and about how to lead the interaction towards effective learning. This isn't easy. They also have to think about what other pupils who are listening to the interaction will be making of it and how to enhance their learning. Public recognition that draws unwelcome attention to failings in pupil performance may be undesirable in many situations.

Pupils' self-confidence is an important factor in the effectiveness of their learning and the way feedback is given and the type of feedback given affects the way they see themselves as learners. If the feedback does not recognise what they *have* achieved and simply focuses on what they *have not* then pupils can find it difficult to see much point in trying harder. Feedback that offers them suggested steps to improve their work encourages them to take those steps. All learners benefit from seeing a way forward that improves what they do, and having confidence in themselves is an important part of that.

A final note that emphasises the complexity of giving feedback comes from the research quoted earlier in the book, which found that merely giving praise did not improve performance. Effective feedback is directed towards improving performance, which in turn helps improve confidence. Trying to improve confidence and hoping that this will improve performance will not be so successful.

How can teacher record keeping be linked to feedback?

Mark books full of marks out of 10 or lists of VG, G, S etc. may be a useful shorthand for performance. However, this form of record keeping needs careful thought. What do the records really mean in terms of pupils' learning? They almost inevitably become removed from the tasks originally set and turn into a broad overall view of pupils 'doing well' or 'doing less well'. This may not be very useful to pupils, because it doesn't clearly identify current understanding or weaknesses or suggest how improvements could be made. When giving feedback to pupils these aspects need to be emphasised and teachers might want to consider whether 'mark' books can be used for recording feedback comments or targets as well as or instead of marks. Again the problem of time and manageability is important here and the issues will be different for primary and secondary teachers.

The important time-management issue is how best to record some of the much wider bank of evidence about pupils that teachers will hold in their heads. The implications are that teachers should think carefully about the information they need to record and how to do this most efficiently, recognising that feedback to pupils needs to take a very different form, because the purpose is different.

What can teachers do to make feedback more effective?

So what can teachers do to make all the time spent marking and providing feedback more effective in terms of learning? In teachers' busy days there is no time for wasted effort. This final section of the chapter will suggest some general strategies for making feedback more effective. We pick up some of the issues already discussed and suggest strategies to make feedback a positive experience that helps learning.

Training pupils to use feedback

Perhaps an obvious place to start is with the pupils themselves. As already shown, teachers should not assume that pupils automatically understand and can make use of feedback. Helping pupils understand how their work has been marked and what they should do with the feedback given is a good investment of time in the long term. Pupils also need to be provided with opportunities and time to implement the suggestions made for improvement of their work. Returning to previous feedback and commenting on how well it has been followed up can reinforce learning.

Grades and links to objectives

The issues associated with grades and feedback have already been outlined. The most important is the effect on performance of giving grades and the meaning pupils associate with them.

*   Comments that focus on the task and its learning objectives, and offer positive ways for pupils to improve their work, are likely to be more helpful than grades.
*   Learning objectives can often usefully be linked to the National Curriculum level descriptions, but they should be written in 'pupil speak'.
*   Most level descriptions are very broad so for individual pieces of work teachers can usefully focus on limited areas within them and resist the temptation to use the level numbers as shorthand. For example, someone learning to cook would not expect to be told, 'That sauce rates a Level 4'. They would want advice on its flavour and texture and what they could do to improve it.

Strategies for test feedback

All pupils do tests from time to time and are always keen to hear their results. 'What did I get?' is their main concern, closely followed by what their friends and others 'got'. The emphasis is always on the mark or grade and seldom do pupils really care about what they actually achieved. How can this become a more valuable learning experience? This is another area in which it is important to change pupils' expectations – and this isn't an easy task. They have deeply held beliefs, which grow up through their experiences of schooling, about the purposes of tests. These do not usually include learning. This doesn't mean that pupils' beliefs can't be changed and tests used in a more productive way.

If the test is being used 'for' learning, it can be used to diagnose areas of weakness and motivate pupils to look at those areas more carefully. For example, test papers can be returned marked but ungraded and pupils can be asked to rework the parts they found difficult using the comments provided. This will motivate them to return to poorly answered questions and to try to understand how to improve their answers, so that their final 'grade' is improved.

Another approach is to ask pupils to work in groups with their marked papers to generate improved answers to a selection of questions. These can then be presented to the rest of the class. Both of these strategies are aiming to integrate 'the test' into the learning so that pupils see it as an opportunity to learn more, rather than simply an ordeal to be got through as quickly as possible. Both strategies thus have a formative purpose, using the test as a motivator, not as a summative judgement.

Timing

Feedback should be given as soon as possible after the work has been completed and it should be in a form that can be acted on in a short time scale. Teachers know these two principles are important but may not always act on them under pressure. The first relates to the needs of the learner to have the work fresh in their mind when they return to think about it again. The second can be more difficult to implement and raises questions about what is useful feedback at particular points. If the particular topic is finished there is little value in detailed feedback, which is not relevant to what a pupil is thinking about now. Time must be made for feedback to be followed up in some way, or it is a waste of time giving it.

Should teachers in a school all mark work in the same way?

Pupils are often very confused about feedback when it comes in different forms from different teachers. This problem is particularly associated with grades and marks, which some research has shown to be a less effective form of feedback anyway.

One answer to this problem is for schools or departments to agree that feedback will only be given in the form of comments directly related to the learning aims; the differences will then just depend on the kind of work being done. This might be a difficult policy to implement but, based on the evidence, would seem to be one that will help pupils make sense of their learning progress.

Verbal feedback

This kind of feedback is often the most valuable for pupils because it allows them to clarify points they don't understand and get really personal attention from their teacher. The trouble is there is only one teacher and lots of pupils.

If ways can be found to make time for individual feedback, which pupils can immediately use in their work, verbal feedback can be more productive. There are inescapable links here with how classrooms are organised and the work that goes on in them. The more ways that can be found to help pupils be independent learners, the more time can be made to have individual discussions with them. This does not mean rushing round the classroom to make sure everyone has been seen; it needs to be more closely tied in to ongoing work patterns. By being selective and having discussions with individuals and small groups at critical moments rather than going for blanket coverage teachers can make this more manageable.

Effects on lower achievers

It appears that teachers find it more difficult to find effective ways of communicating with lower-achieving and more poorly motivated pupils. Certainly, many of these pupils are less effective at using feedback. The research evidence suggests feedback is more likely to tell them an answer rather than prompt about how to work towards one for themselves. Teachers often give them less information about what they are trying to achieve, perhaps believing that they shouldn't be 'over-loaded' with information they may not understand. All this makes it very difficult for them to work as informed learners, understanding what they are trying to achieve even when they cannot yet achieve it.

This re-emphasises the need for effective communication between teacher and pupils and between pupils. Teachers can make sure the learning objectives of activities are understood, by working with them in the classroom and encouraging pupils to interpret them for them-selves or in groups (another form of advanced organiser). Ensuring that pupils are told 'By the end of this lesson/week you will . . .' and then spending time at the end of the lesson/week checking what has been learnt and asking pupils to evaluate their learning for themselves can be a valuable starting point.

Target-setting

Target-setting (see Chapter 3) has been found to be a helpful way of enhancing achievement. If pupils are clear about what they are trying to achieve, feedback has a powerful role in commenting on the level of their success and how to improve this. Feedback needs to be very directly targeted towards the particular goals concerned, and targets set should be agreed, specific, challenging and followed up.

Being clear about purposes

Feedback has different purposes at different times and if teachers know why they are giving a particular piece of feedback, it is likely to be more successful. For example, is the purpose

- to discuss some written feedback or for pupils to read it independently?
- to get pupils to work further on an existing piece of work or to carry out another piece of work in which they will implement the feedback given?
- to use the piece of work and its feedback to record a particular achievement of a pupil?
- to communicate with parents through the feedback given?

The decisions made about purpose affect the form of the feedback given.

Some guidelines for giving feedback

We finish with part of a set of guidelines about giving feedback from David Boud (1995). These guidelines were designed for those giving feedback to peers, but they apply just as well to teachers giving feedback. Some may need expansion (see the References if you are interested in where to find Boud's writing on this) and are worth trying. What is important is what they mean to the person using them.

- Be realistic.
- Be specific.
- Be sensitive to the goals of the person.
- Be timely.
- Be descriptive.
- Be consciously non-judgemental.
- Don't compare.
- Be diligent.
- Be direct.
- Be positive.
- Be aware.

Conclusion

Marking and feedback are important elements in teaching and learning and take up a considerable amount of teachers' time. To be most effective they should be integral to the teaching and learning process, so that the assessment contributes to learning. We therefore suggest that for marking and feedback to be most effective:

- schools and teachers need to consider why and how work is marked
- schools and teachers should consider the role of grades and comments in helping pupils learn, since the research suggests that comments are more effective than grades
- teachers should prioritise their marking to ensure that it is manageable

- teachers should ensure the information collected and recorded meets the different needs of providing feedback and recording/certifying progress
- tasks need clear purposes and outcomes, which are shared with the pupils
- marking needs clear criteria, which are shared with the pupils
- feedback should help pupils understand how successful they have been
- feedback should tell pupils what they have to do next to improve their work
- feedback should be a motivator; it should both support and challenge pupils
- teachers should remember that feedback can have significant effects on pupils' self-esteem.

ACTIVITIES

1   Looking at the types of marking used and feedback given

Collect some pupils' work which you have marked. What marking criteria did you use? Were these shared with the pupils?

Look at the feedback you gave. Did you use marks? If so, how? Are they 'quantitative', perhaps a mark out of 10, or 'qualitative', for example 'very good'?

How does the feedback link with the objectives of the work? Is it explicit? Does it help pupils understand how to 'bridge the gap'?

2   Working with comments

Spend a few minutes with a pupil talking about the feedback you have given on some pieces of work. What does the pupil understand by it? What use has the pupil made of it? Think about whether this was what you intended and how you could make your feedback more useful.

Try this activity with pupils of different attainment levels. Often lower achievers find feedback much harder to use than higher attainers. How does our feedback need to vary so that all pupils can use it effectively?

3   Learning to use feedback

Decide on a way of following up feedback with a group of pupils. This will depend on the topic and pupils involved but should include some active, immediate use of the feedback by the pupils. Spend some time in a lesson explaining this to pupils and carrying it out. Follow it up in future responses to their work. ·

Do you notice any change in the pupils' approach to feedback? Are they more able to make use of it effectively? You'll need to maintain the momentum!

4   Making tests into learning opportunities

When giving a test to a class discuss with them beforehand how you intend to use it afterwards. Remind them that its purpose is to help them learn more about the topic and that you will be working after the test on this as well as before.

Use one of the strategies in this chapter, or a suitable adaptation, to work with the test outcomes after pupils have formally sat the test.

How effective is this as a way of engaging with errors or misconceptions? Do some pupils learn more about the test topic? What are the problems with the way you chose and how could you adapt your strategy next time to make it work better?

You could do this with some of the end-of-key-stage tests.

5   Getting the timing right

Look back over the last few weeks and think about the extent to which you have achieved the two principles of timing of feedback given above.

What can you do to improve this? You are not trying to make things more difficult for yourself, so don't set yourself tighter and more inflexible timetables for returning work to pupils. Think more creatively.

Try giving feedback at different times, so that pupils have more time to work with it. Try reducing the amount of written feedback so that it can be given more quickly. Try being selective about what you give feedback on.

6 Developing assessment for learning

> Promoting children's learning is a principal aim of schools. Assessment lies at the heart of this process. It can provide a framework in which educational objectives may be set, and pupils' progress charted and expressed. It can yield a basis for planning the next educational steps in response to children's needs.
>
> (DES/WO, 1988: para. 3)

We have argued throughout this book that research shows standards can be raised if assessment promotes learning – if it is assessment *for* learning. We have also suggested that the current 'measurement' culture in England and Wales places too much emphasis on assessment as collecting 'evidence' *of* learning and not enough on using assessment to plan for children's future learning needs. While the measurement culture has undoubtedly resulted in a rise in 'test scores' we suggest greater gains could be achieved if assessment for learning were used more widely and effectively.

In this chapter we consider how schools can develop their assessment practice in the light of the significant research findings outlined in the rest of this book. We make suggestions of strategies and techniques that schools and teachers can discuss and try out. These are not ready-made, 'off-the-shelf' instant solutions to raising standards that will work for everyone. Some will work in your school, with your teachers and pupils, others won't. The research asks questions and can suggest routes to explore, but the issues are complex and the contexts are different. Change will take time and may be frustrating. However, what is clear from the research is that a number of key factors can help teachers use assessment to promote learning.

Achievement can be raised if teachers:

* plan carefully
* have clear learning intentions
* believe in their pupils
* give appropriate feedback
* involve pupils in the assessment process.

How can schools use assessment to enhance teaching and learning?

We explore four key areas in this chapter:

* how *policies* can be used as a tool for change
* how *planning* for assessment can improve teaching and learning
* how to develop different methods of *collecting and analysing* assessment data
* how to *record and report* achievement for different purposes.

Table 6.1 identifies some questions schools can ask about each of these four key areas of change and the opportunities for *action* in each area.

How policies can be used as a tool for change

Schools often start to review current practice by asking three questions:

* Where are we now?
* Where do we want to be?
* How will we get there?

If these are used to review current assessment practice throughout the school, similarities and differences in practice can be identified, reasons for successes and failures analysed and other ways of working identified. The results can lead to a draft plan for action that suits the needs of the school. After consultation this plan can become part of the school development plan and form the basis of the agreed school policy on assessment.

Table 6.1 Key areas for developing assessment

Area	Questions to consider	Possible action
Policy	Reviewing assessment practice/policies • Where are we now? • Where do we want to be? • How will we get there? Developing assessment practice	Conduct audit of current practice/policies. Establish working group to develop assessment.
Planning	Learning objectives • What do I want the pupils to learn? Learning activities • How will they learn it? Planning assessment opportunities (formal and informal) • How will I know when they've learned it?	Identify clear objectives. Plan learning activities with assessment in mind and clear criteria that assess learning not behaviour.
Assessing	Using existing information • What do I already know about the pupils? Collecting assessment evidence • How can I find out more?	Sources of evidence. Looking, listening, observing, testing, marking.
Analysing	Professional judgements • What do the pupils know and understand? • What can they do? Self-assessment • How well do pupils think they are doing?	Shared understanding of achievement. Develop strategies for self/peer assessment.
Targets	• What happens next?	Agree SMART targets and action plans.
Recording	• What do I need to record in terms of significant progress? • How do I record assessment information?	Ongoing marks and recorded comments. Outcomes of special assessment tasks.
Reporting	• Who needs to know this information? • What form should it take?	Parents, other teachers Reports, RoA, portfolios of students' work, summative records

Source: Adapted from Butt *et al.* (1995)

Current practice

Policies are a useful management tool for schools, but in many cases their influence on practice is limited. In 1984 research conducted by the National Foundation for Educational Research (NFER) found that assessment policies, if written down at all, were limited in scope and unclear about purposes and principles. Their focus tended to be on how work would be marked and how assessments would be structured during the year; they emphasised collecting and recording data about students so they could be graded and compared. There were few comments about the power of formative assessment that has been the major theme of this book.

More recently Mary James (1998: 9–13) conducted an informal review of 20 OFSTED reports relating to secondary and middle schools inspected in 1994–5. She found a number of themes that are worth considering.

Format and content

Schools generally had (often recently written) assessment policies. Only some policies had a rationale and many were restricted to 'marking' and 'prescriptions' for practice.

Implementation

There was little evidence that assessment, recording and reporting were being used to monitor students' progress and to inform planning of teaching and learning.

In all schools inspectors noted inconsistency in the implementation of policies both between and within departments and between key stages. There was little evidence of moderation arrangements to improve this position and only limited evidence of the use of portfolios of exemplar material.

Grading scales were common, encouraging norm-referencing, and they were often unrelated to National Curriculum or examination standards, so that pupils had little understanding of the standards required.

Comments on students' work were very variable in content and quality. Too often, according to the inspectors, narrative comments related to attitude, effort and behaviour but neglected to evaluate learning in terms of knowledge, skill and understanding.

Self-assessment and target-setting

In a few schools self-assessment, review and action planning had been introduced, often in association with the development of records of achievement. Where this process occurred, it was valued by students but it was unclear whether the process contributed formatively to their learning.

Review and planning

Most schools had begun to analyse test and examination data but there was little evidence that the data was used to identify areas for improvement.

The highest praise went to schools where assessment, recording and reporting had been a priority for the school development plan and where the responsibility had been delegated to a member of senior management who was supported by a working group.

Can policies be used to encourage change?

While Mary James's evidence is from a small sample it suggests that schools in 1994–5 had a limited view of an assessment policy and failed to use it as part of their review and planning mechanism. They were not using policies as an agent of change. We suggest that to make significant changes assessment and raising standards have to be a priority on the school's development plan and be supported by effective mechanisms for change.

Managing change

There has been copious research on the management of change, but the findings haven't necessarily been used effectively in schools. Michael Fullan (1991) has pointed out that many people (politicians and headteachers included) think that once a policy has been created the hard work has been done. He quotes an outgoing deputy minister of education talking to a colleague: 'Well the hard work is done. We have the policy passed; now all you have to do is implement it' (Fullan, 1991: 65).

We suggest that it's not as easy as that. Changing practice in the classroom is a process, not an event, and needs time and support for those undertaking the change. This may be why the most effective schools, as reported by Mary James, had a delegated senior member of staff and a working party implementing their changes.

Michael Fullan also suggests that many educational innovations have been frustrated by the inherent but understandable 'conservatism' of teachers. He suggests that real change will only occur where teacher beliefs about teaching and learning have been significantly altered. Education is littered with examples of innovations that have either failed or only been partially implemented because teachers weren't convinced the change was necessary and would result in real improvement. The result has been that they merely modify their practice at the edges and then abandon the change after a while because it 'didn't work for them'. More effective use of assessment, particularly formative assessment, will require many teachers to reconsider their approach to teaching and learning and to re-evaluate their working practices.

If schools and teachers want to make changes they have to be committed to continually re-examining their ways of working and their underlying beliefs about teaching and learning. Real educational change requires more than the 'quick-fix' solution of the inspirational educational 'guru' or the educational recipe book. It requires schools and teachers to become 'researchers' in their own classrooms, to identify problems, seek solutions, try them out and analyse the outcomes. The most effective schools promote this questioning and learning environment and encourage teachers to share their work in a supportive but challenging learning environment. Demonstrating that 'it works' is a powerful agent of change. If some teachers make changes and demonstrate that their classes have made significant progress, then other teachers are more likely to follow.

It is worth considering a long-term plan that starts by involving a small number of teachers who carry out an initial research programme. Increasingly there are mechanisms to support this research, for example funding from the DfES Best Practice Research Studentships which are linked to support from researchers in local HEIs. The results can be shared most effectively through a working group reviewing assessment policy and practice, because the group acts both as catalyst and support for individuals or groups of teachers introducing new ideas into their classrooms.

How can policies be made more effective agents of change?

Format, content, review and planning

The most effective policies will be brief 'working' documents that have a clear rationale stating the different diagnostic, formative, summative and evaluative purposes of assessment within the school and providing an agreed framework that goes beyond 'marking' and 'prescriptions' for practice. The policy should be reviewed on a regular basis and should inform teachers' planning, although detail about implementation may not be necessary.

Implementation

It is important to consider how the assessment policy is implemented on a whole-school basis. Issues such as using assessment data more effectively, achieving consistency and whether to use grades and/or comments have important implications for all teachers' practice.

The potential of assessment, recording and reporting is often under-used. The data available can be used for broad evaluative purposes and also to monitor students' progress and to inform teachers' planning. The increasing amounts of data available to schools, through PANDAs (Performance and Assessment reports) or information systems such as Pips, Midyis, Yellis and Alis are a valuable source of information for identifying potential under-achievement. Many schools are using this data successfully to monitor and target individual pupils. However, beware of labelling pupils. There is much evidence to suggest that performance in one assessment is not necessarily a good predictor of future achievement. With any 'labelling' as a result of assessment there is a danger that pupils live 'up' or 'down' to that expectation.

Many schools have tried to rationalise the wide variety of assessment practice that exists although consistent practice can be difficult to achieve, particularly in large schools, and in some cases there may be valid reasons for differences. One method of improving consistency is to have effective, regular moderation procedures, including the use of portfolios of exemplar material. Moderation also allows teachers to share good practice and is a form of professional development. Sharing the assessment policy with pupils is good practice and can be achieved by displaying expectations on walls and in books. However, remember the best systems are open to interpretation by teachers who may still implement the policy in idiosyncratic ways and pupils' perceptions will have to be regularly checked to ensure they understand how their work is being assessed.

Marking – grades or comments?

Marking is always an issue for schools. Many teachers have sat through departmental or staff meetings where assessment practice has been discussed and ended up realising that there are almost as many different ways of marking as there are people in the room.

The value of comments in promoting learning, rather than marks or grades which can be a barrier to learning, has been explored in Chapter 5. This is likely to be an area where the issues need to be discussed widely and some pilot studies carried out in the school as many teachers may be reluctant to change their practice.

Whatever marking system is used it is worth remembering that all pupils need clear guidance on where they are, what they have to do next and how to improve. The most successful teachers have always done this by focusing on what the pupil knows and can do, rather than commenting on attitude, effort or behaviour.

Self-assessment and target-setting

In Chapter 4 we suggested that self-assessment and target-setting are powerful tools that can help pupils identify and understand what they need to do to raise their achievement. However, they may be unfamiliar to many pupils and probably work best when the whole school culture supports them. One aspect of a school assessment policy might therefore be to promote a culture where regular self-assessment and target-setting is carried out at all levels of the school.

Action points – using assessment policies to raise standards

To summarise, a number of actions at the policy or whole-school level can contribute to raising standards:

- Policies should be working documents that inform practice.
- Assessment should have targets within the school development plan.
- A member of the SMT (senior management team) supported by a working group should have ongoing responsibility for reviewing assessment policy and practice.
- Innovation in assessment practice should be encouraged, supported and evaluated.
- Teacher comments should focus on pupil learning more than attitude, effort and behaviour.
- The use of marks or grades should be carefully reviewed.
- Ways of sharing assessment criteria with pupils should be explored and evaluated.
- Moderation systems that improve consistency of judgements should be in place.

How planning for assessment can improve teaching and learning

Long-, medium- and short-term planning all play an important part in the process of helping pupils learn more effectively and thereby raise standards. While teachers have increasingly committed their long- and medium-term plans to paper in schemes of work that outline teaching and learning intentions (what, how, when and with what resources), these schemes of work often have an assessment opportunities column that is under-used or insufficiently focused. This is a missed opportunity because at its best this column clearly identifies learning intentions that can be translated into activities in the classroom through short-term lesson plans.

Identifying learning intentions

Identifying clear learning intentions is a vital part of planning for assessment, because they give a focus to the lesson that can be shared

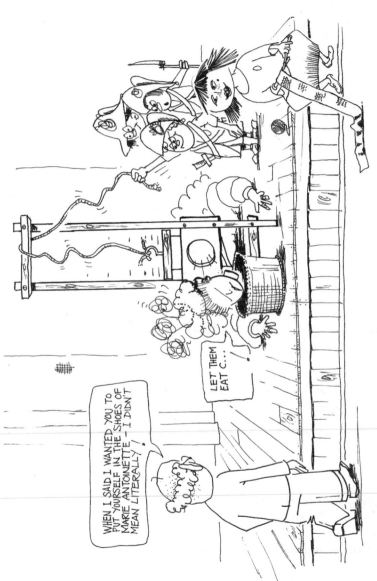

Figure 6.1 The well-planned lesson includes an opportunity for assessment

with the pupils at the start and evaluated at the end. However, it appears that many teachers find them difficult to formulate. Too often planning involves broad sweeping aims and imprecise outcomes or focuses merely on content rather than identifying what is required in terms of pupil learning or outcomes.

For example, 'graphs' does not sufficiently indicate the learning intention. 'Being able to plot data accurately onto a prepared line graph' is better because it indicates more clearly the fact that it is the skill of graph drawing that is being developed and the level of the skill expected is indicated.

> Properly planned and co-ordinated assessment activity . . . helps to develop a collective view of assessment, a shared expertise in the planning of teaching and assessment, and an agreed understanding of standards, expectations and pupils' achievements throughout the school. These can provide helpful support to teachers when they make the judgements at the end of a key stage.
>
> (SCAA 1995: 5)

As this quotation suggests, planning assessment activities that have identified intentions and outcomes is also beneficial for professional development, because it encourages teachers to share their understanding of standards.

Action points – using planning to promote assessment

Table 6.2 shows how the different stages of planning require different levels of detail about assessment approaches. Planning should be reviewed regularly to ensure that the intentions are being achieved.

How to develop different methods of collecting and analysing assessment data

Classroom assessment – the role of the teacher

Teachers make judgements about pupils all the time. They comment that this child is quiet, this one is hardworking, this one is lively, but

Table 6.2 Planning for assessment

Stage of planning	Purpose	Content/assessment opportunities
Long term (curriculum overview – yearly or key stage)	Outlines coverage. Identifies breadth, balance, continuity and progression.	Summary of subject content for each term/half term for each year group. Broad overview of 'formal' and 'informal' assessment opportunities.
Medium term (termly or half termly)	Teaching framework for the term, half term or module. Will be more or less specific depending on the school context (e.g. use by non-specialist teachers, NQTs, supply teachers) but should be flexible enough to allow adaptation.	Shows clear learning intentions and an overview of activities. Identifies clear assessment opportunities and may indicate the range of pupil standards/expectations.
Short term (weekly or daily)	Teacher's personal agenda for the week's lessons. Identifies assessment opportunities and allows day to day assessment judgements to be recorded. Opportunities for lessons to be modified in the light of these judgements.	Should include: • specific learning intentions • activities • organisation/ differentiation • provision for SEN • rough time allocations • assessment notes.

these are comments about attitudes and behaviour not learning and attainment. How can teachers really know what the child knows, understands and can do? If they find that five children can do a task, while the rest of the class, to varying degrees, are struggling, how can they use this information to plan future lessons? Are the judgements made accurate and do they truly reflect pupils' abilities or is more evidence needed?

Using existing information

If teachers receive assessment data from other teachers or from formal assessments, do they use this information to differentiate between pupils? The transfer from KS2 to KS3 is particularly problematic, with many children failing to make progress for some time after the transfer. Common comments from secondary teachers are: 'I want to start with a clean slate so that I don't prejudge the children'; 'The pupils have had such different experiences we have to start from the lowest common point'; 'I haven't got time to read all the information I receive'. This results in many pupils doing inappropriate work, either too hard or too easy, which can have consequences for motivation, self-image and learning.

Collecting assessment evidence

The key issue here is that any judgement must be tentative and teachers should always be looking to find out more about their pupils. To do this it is useful for teachers to have three questions at the back of their minds:

- What do the pupils already know?
- How can I find out more about their learning?
- How will this information help me plan or adapt this lesson or future lessons?

Within a lesson there are many opportunities to collect snippets of assessment information and to begin to make tentative judgements about pupils and learning.

At the start of the lesson the teacher had displayed three words that the pupils were to learn during the lesson and the three key ideas they were going to study. She started by asking how many pupils had heard of ___ Several hands went up and she got responses from three or four of them. When an answer needed clarifying she asked for more information or justification. Later in the lesson all the pupils were asked to write three things they knew about ___

The third activity required the pupils to read a passage of text and answer some comprehension questions. At the end of the lesson there was another question and answer session where understanding of the key ideas of the lesson were checked.

This teacher had been presented with a mass of information about the pupils – too much to take in while she was also concentrating on managing the lesson effectively. However, some parts of the lesson were more structured towards identifying how much individuals knew or had learnt and she stored this information for use later on when planning the next lesson. Particularly interesting pieces of information that challenged her previous judgements of pupils were recorded on her lesson plan. Recording of evidence is important and will be discussed later. How can the mass of information available be filtered and recorded in manageable ways?

Methods of gathering assessment evidence and analysing it

There are many ways of gathering evidence for assessment and analysing it, with the methods used varying by subject and pupil age. A number of methods commonly used are identified in Table 6.3 and some will be discussed more fully. In this section we concentrate on how the data can be collected and analysed while methods of recording are discussed later. Some assessment opportunities will occur routinely, while others need more careful planning.

Observation

This is probably the most frequently used method in the classroom and yet is possibly the least recognised as a form of assessment. In everyday life we constantly make judgements about people and draw inferences, often based on very little evidence. The process of observing, inferring, judging and deciding can be almost instantaneous and a teacher's initial impressions may need to be modified as they find out more. In a teaching situation, teachers need to be conscious that they are making

Table 6.3 A typology of assessment data-gathering methods

	Looking	*Listening*	*Asking*
Routinely occurring	Observation Marking pupils' work	Active listening	Questioning Setting tasks Subject-based tests
		Discussion Oral assessment Conferencing	
	Assessing practical competence		
Specially undertaken	Systematic observation	Audio recording	Interviewing Questionnaires Examining Cognitive testing
	Video recording		

Source: Adapted from Pollard and Triggs (1997)

judgements and develop ways of checking that the judgement is accurate, so that actions based on these judgements are the most appropriate for their pupils. For example, it may be necessary to resist the temptation to say John is lazy, because his writing is poor and he rarely gets anything down on paper. He may have a specific learning difficulty, such as dyslexia, which is causing him to have difficulty with both his reading and writing.

Teachers also need to remember the 'invisible' pupils in their classes, with whom they may have few direct interactions and about whom they feel they have less personal knowledge. Do not assume that Kelly is 'slow' because she doesn't talk in class. She may be learning more by listening than pupils who always answer. To make an accurate judgement she will need to be targeted more directly, maybe by other methods.

Observation will therefore need to be systematic, focusing on individual children and particular behaviours so that a clearer, more accurate picture is gained. It is not practical to do this for every child all the time, but careful planning can build in observation opportunities that are used to check inferences and judgements from other sources of evidence.

Questioning, listening and discussion

These are three of the most important and natural ways by which teachers form assessment judgements, particularly of individual pupils. The great advantages of questioning, listening and discussion are that they are immediate, interactive and can be used for both formative and summative purposes. Potentially, then, they are amongst the most sensitive, subtle and useful skills in any teacher's teaching and assessment repertoire.

However, using questions effectively is a skill that needs practice and there is considerable research evidence that teachers limit questions to recall, use them more for class management and fail to develop the sort of extended questioning sequence that enables knowledge and understanding to be developed. Another problem arises from the transient nature of the situation – how does a teacher record information gained from pupils' responses while conducting the session? The answer to this has to be that it is done at the first opportunity afterwards, maybe on the lesson plan, so that when reviewing and planning future work it is there as a stimulus to jog the memory.

Oral assessment

One related area is the use of oral assessment to assess knowledge, understanding and the use of language. Oral assessment may be particularly useful with younger pupils, or pupils with specific learning difficulties, such as dyslexia, whose written skills are poor. It is also important for assessing verbal communication skills. In these circumstances, it allows the teacher to check knowledge and understanding in an extremely flexible manner.

Oral assessment can also be used to aid learning through role play or discussions. Presentations or debates may provide useful insights for teachers and open the way for further questioning which allows the teacher to explore knowledge, understanding and the development of thinking in a detailed and comprehensive manner. Again methods of recording evidence need to be considered beforehand.

Figure 6.2 Effective questioning

Setting tasks

Teachers set pupils tasks to perform on a daily basis, which provide a valuable source of evidence of pupil learning. Teachers who are aware of the importance of formative assessment and of the potential for gathering evidence from everyday classroom activities should be able to focus the tasks so that pupil actions and performance reveal what they know, can do and understand. The teacher's skill lies in setting tasks that are appropriate and accessible for all the pupils but which also highlight what particular pupils have learned. Sometimes pupil understanding can best be checked by the use of 'trick' questions that expose pupil misconceptions.

Using everyday tasks for assessment purposes means that the opportunities are frequent and routine and the validity is likely to be high. Since the task is embedded in everyday classroom processes, it should provide a rich source of insights about pupil learning strategies and attainments, which can be used formatively. A note of caution, however. The assessment purpose of a task must be planned and should be shared with the pupils. It is clear from the research that classroom tasks are often merely recall or comprehension activities that may provide little useful assessment data. Further, when introducing tasks, teachers are better at telling pupils what they have to do than why they are doing the task and how it will help their learning.

Marking

Marking has already been discussed in detail in Chapter 5, so here we focus on how marking provides assessment data. The most common way for teachers to monitor pupils' learning is to 'mark' work which has been completed, either in class or for homework. To be most useful, marking should be done as soon as possible after the work is completed, with the pupil present, so when feedback is given, the work is fresh in the pupil's mind.

However, for practical reasons, marking is often done by the teacher in the absence of the pupil concerned, so there is no opportunity to talk with them and find out how they set about the task or to check misunderstandings. In such cases, marking can become more summative than diagnostic and may be less useful for planning next steps in learning.

Marking can easily become focused on what can be measured in a straightforward way, ignoring more amorphous but potentially more important areas. The LEARN project found that pupils were aware that they might be assessed on their spelling and getting sums correct but were less sure about how quality of work would be 'measured' (as are many teachers). Thus a large area of potential data may be overlooked because teachers find identifying and using the criteria difficult and time-consuming.

Marking can be used in conjunction with other forms of monitoring. For instance, teacher judgement when marking is often informed by observations – as when the teacher circulates around the room during classwork – and also by discussions which may have taken place during lessons.

Self-assessment

Self-assessment, as discussed in Chapter 4, can provide useful insights into pupils' thinking about their work and the effort they have put into it. This is a valuable activity (not just to save teachers' time!), since it helps develop pupils' understanding of the work they are doing and of its underlying purposes. The skill of marking their own work is one which pupils need to practise. Pupils are often very 'hard' on themselves and some do not find it easy to interpret their work flexibly if it does not precisely match the criteria in the 'mark scheme'. They benefit from having questions to help guide their assessment. Some examples are: What have you learnt? What is good about this work? What could you improve? These questions can be adapted to focus on particular areas that the teacher wants to know more about.

Conferencing, action planning and progress review

These are terms used to describe forms of extended discussion, usually with specific goals and outcomes, which take place between teachers and pupils. Such sessions offer an opportunity for a teacher and pupil to come to a mutual understanding concerning an issue which has arisen (conferencing), to agree future learning or behavioural targets (action planning) or to discuss the outcomes of previous efforts (progress review).

Of course, the in-depth discussions which are involved in conferencing, action planning and progress review could pose management problems for any teacher. How to fit in necessary discussions? What preparation is necessary? What will other pupils be doing while the teacher is thus engaged? The length of the discussions will vary with the needs of the pupil and the wise teacher will plan to set aside a certain amount of time, perhaps during a set lesson period, when the class knows that the teacher–pupil discussion must not be interrupted, if at all possible. The balance between teacher and pupil talking is also important as teachers can dominate a conversation and it is important that they listen to what the pupil has to say. Pupils should be encouraged to identify their own strengths, weaknesses and targets.

For some topics, discussions with a group might be appropriate, and collective action plans or targets could result. However, it is important that a group context does not inhibit some of the more reticent individuals.

Subject-based and cognitive testing

Testing takes many forms and is used for a wide range of purposes. We now identify some of the differences between the main types of test and testing practice and identify ways in which tests can be used to promote learning.

Criterion-referenced / norm-referenced tests

Criterion-referenced tests are concerned with assessing whether each pupil's performance satisfies specified criteria. For instance, in England and Wales the attainment targets that form the national testing regime at key stages 1, 2 and 3 are criteria-based, as are many 'mastery' tests such as graded sports awards, cycling proficiency and vehicle driving tests. While criterion-referenced testing is supposed to be the basis for all statutory assessment activity in England and Wales, research has shown that normative assumptions can creep back into judgements that teachers and others make when carrying out both teacher and standardised assessment procedures. This can mean they assume that some pupils will not meet the standard identified in the criteria. When using criteria it is possible that everyone will 'master' the requirements and teachers can help pupils by clearly identifying how their work could be improved in terms of the criteria.

Norm-referenced tests provide 'standardised' comparisons of individuals in terms of 'normal' expectations of achievement. These are well established through 'IQ tests' and other forms of cognitive measure of verbal or mathematical reasoning. The 'norm' will be the score achieved by half of the population. At present, in England and Wales it appears that normative tests are often regarded as being more reliable than criterion-referenced tests. For example, it is common for secondary schools to ask each new intake of year 7 pupils to take cognitive and/or subject-based forms of norm-referenced tests on entry, despite having key stage 2 criterion-referenced data. We would argue that neither is necessarily better – they are almost certainly assessing different aspects of a pupil's attainment and provide useful evidence that helps build a more complete picture. All the information can be used to identify strengths and weaknesses and help in the setting of future targets.

Whatever type of test is used, teachers should be aware that it may have limitations. They should try to identify its strengths, weaknesses and underlying assumptions about learning. We cannot assume that any test is perfect, and should ask a number of questions about it.

• Is the test founded on an appropriate conceptualisation of learning?
• Does the test generate valid data?
• Does it really measure what it is supposed to measure?
• Can the test be used reliably so that results are consistent?

Teacher tests / published tests

Tests which teachers devise themselves and which are directly related to what has been taught may be contrasted with published tests which are intended to be generally applicable to a wide range of situations. Teacher tests are widely used for diagnostic purposes to assess the extent to which pupils have learned a particular, locally developed unit of work. They can also be used to assess a teacher's effectiveness in implementing specified learning objectives. Unfortunately the evidence suggests that often they merely emphasise recall of knowledge or imitate summative assessments.

Many publishers now produce assessments in conjunction with textbooks. These are most useful where the data provides clear evidence of learning or misconceptions by individuals or groups so that future activities can be planned. As with any test, an overall mark does not help a pupil know where they went wrong. This has to be teased out by the teacher, which may be time-consuming.

Open-response / closed-response tests

Many classroom tests pose questions in which there is room for imagination and creativity, such as an essay, review, synopsis, investigation or problem-solving task. Such open-response tests are particularly common in English and the humanities, but these subjects may also use closed tests in relation to issues such as spelling, dates, capital cities or other forms of factual information. Closed-response tests presume that there is one right answer, and multiple-choice questions, with selection between pre-specified answers, are an extreme example of this. Information about misconceptions or general areas of weakness can be gained from both types of test, but tends to be richer in quality from open-response tests.

Computer-based tests

These are becoming increasingly common. The best identify areas of strength and weakness, quickly giving either the teacher or the pupil a diagnosis of problems. This information can then be used as the basis for planning future work. The speed of analysis makes them a useful diagnostic tool if the questions go beyond recall, comprehension and skills to identify understanding and synthesis.

Public examinations

Can public examinations be a source of assessment data? Yes, and that data can be of use to both teachers and pupils. Of course, public examinations are very different from most of the other forms of assessment which have been discussed in this chapter because teachers essentially begin to lose control of the process. In the past this process used to be hidden but increasingly feedback to teachers has enabled them to become more knowledgeable about the exam process and what pupils need to do to achieve success. The issue for teachers is how to share this information with pupils so that they develop better revision and examination techniques.

Action points – collecting and analysing assessment data

Collecting and analysing assessment data is an ongoing process that can be improved if teachers:

- use a variety of different methods
- are clear about the purpose of the assessment
- understand the limitations of the assessment in providing data
- have time to analyse the data effectively
- record evidence in both systematic and ad-hoc ways

- make sure pupils understand the purposes and criteria of the assessment
- involve pupils in the process of collecting and analysing data.

How to record and report achievement for different purposes

Records have different audiences, including pupils, parents, other teachers and external agencies, and different purposes, so the information recorded may need to be in different forms. Useful questions to consider are:

- What is the purpose of recording this information?
- What form should it take?

What is the purpose of recording this information?

Some of the most important purposes for records and reporting are:

- *to inform future teaching*
  Teachers need accurate and relevant information about the pupils in their classes on which they can base their planning. Such records should make it easier to achieve an appropriate match between pupils, curriculum, teaching and learning.

- *to support personal reflection*
  By reviewing records of pupil achievements, particularly in conjunction with a portfolio of work, teachers can reflect on the success of their teaching and can use the information to develop their teaching further.

- *to underpin continuity and progression*
  Records exchanged between teachers provide a crucial means of ensuring that there is continuity and progression in the pupils' learning experiences from year to year or across subject teams. Discussions about how to ensure continuity between different phases within the education system are important. Many departments and schools now keep portfolios of pupils' work for the purpose of agreeing 'levels' for teacher assessment, and engage in

progressive target-setting and action planning with each pupil. Transition between schools can be difficult for many pupils and this can affect the progress of their learning.

- *to contribute to summative assessment and accountability processes*
  Records and evidence of pupil attainments have become increasingly needed for summative assessment and accountability purposes. Such records can be helpful when reporting to parents, but are also likely to be used to compile indicators of teacher, subject department, school or LEA performance.

What form should the record or report take?

Keeping accurate and consistent records is of major significance for schools and is likely to be structured by whole-school policies. Individual classroom teachers can certainly keep whatever personal records they wish, but we suggest this is best framed within an official faculty, subject department or whole-school system. It is vital that information is collected in manageable ways and that it is possible to organise, analyse and use it effectively. Over the years it has been found that inappropriately elaborate and time-consuming systems are likely to be discarded.

Portfolio of student's work

One of the most valuable forms of record is a portfolio of each pupil's work and assessment information, which provides evidence for understanding the development and achievements of the young person. Such portfolios can incorporate material from activities such as classwork, homework, class tests, cognitive tests and end of year examinations, and they provide an excellent resource for reviewing progress and target-setting.

Keeping a record of ongoing marks and comments

There is a range of alternative forms in which records could be kept. For example, personal teacher records may simply be jotted in an exercise book. More formal records for faculty, department or whole-school systems are likely to be recorded with a standardised pro-forma employed by all staff. A variety of standardised sheets are provided by LEAs, publishers, exam boards and accreditation agencies, but many schools prefer to devise their own formats to reflect their particular circumstances. A more elaborate method is to put pupil information onto a computer database, where it can be easily updated and quickly accessed. In addition to providing normal access to parents, such databases must be registered appropriately, in England, under the terms of the Data Protection Act 1985.

Reporting to parents

Written reports to parents are important documents which contain a range of types of information and have complex purposes. For parents, they are the principal means of obtaining 'official' information about the progress of their children and they also implicitly provide information about the school, its teachers and their values and emphases. If appropriately written, reports can encourage parents to work with teachers and will go a long way towards making an effective relationship to support pupils' learning.

Action points

Record keeping and reporting

*   should consider the audience (pupils, parents, other teachers and external agencies)
*   should take a form appropriate to the audience
*   should be appropriate to the purpose (future planning, personal reflection, progression and continuity, accountability).

Conclusion

As we have argued throughout this book, assessment has been, and remains, a controversial issue in education. It has been seen as a very important element of public education policy that is often used as a means of raising standards of pupil attainment. We suggest however that pupils need more than measurement if they are going to make progress. The skill of the teacher is required to plan assessment opportunities, to collect and analyse data and provide ongoing feedback that helps pupils understand where they are going, where they are now, and how to 'bridge the gap' between the two.

This chapter has examined some ways in which teachers can improve their practice in relation to the fundamental question: how do we 'know' what each pupil knows, understands and can do? Throughout we have suggested that any judgement we make must inevitably be tentative and subject to revision in the light of new evidence. As Patricia Broadfoot (1996) suggests, 'educational assessment can never be scientific' because of its interpersonal characteristics and the complexity of the variables being measured.

Finally, throughout this book we have argued that professional practice has tended to be shaped by the assessment purposes which have been given priority, and in recent years summative performance measures for pupils and schools have been overemphasised. This chapter has therefore suggested some ways in which formative assessment, placed at the heart of the teaching and learning process, can be central to the day-to-day work of schools.

ACTIVITIES

1   Planning for assessment and recording

Look at your long-, medium- and short-term plans.

How are assessment opportunities identified?

How do you plan to include specific assessment opportunities in a lesson?

How do you share your intentions with the pupils?

How do you record significant information you collect about individuals during a lesson?

2   Mark a pupil's work to identify their achievements and weaknesses

Collect a sequence of work from a pupil. Contrast the early and later work and note the major developments. Then list and prioritise continuing weaknesses.

Talk with the pupil and affirm their progress. Negotiate with the pupil to agree targets for future development.

This is a way to use marking formatively for an individual. Marking the work of the whole class on a particular piece of work is also helpful in identifying aspects which several pupils may need help with or for gauging understanding and competence in the class as a whole.

Look back through your marking. What does each comment tell the pupil? How often is it merely encouraging? How often does it focus on spelling, grammar or neatness? What aspects of the quality of work do you comment on? How often do your comments engage with what the pupil was trying to do?

3   Using target-setting

We suggest that target-setting is initially tried on a relatively small scale, with a few identified pupils, so that it does not take too much time.

Who: Choose pupils with whom you want to negotiate learning targets.

When: Make time for a one-to-one discussion. Decide how you will make time and what the other pupils will be doing.

What: Be clear and specific about the focus for the discussion, and, if possible, agree this with the pupil. Aim for small successes and build on them.

How: How will you discuss the issue with the pupil? How will progress to achieving the target be monitored?

4   Using tests for formative assessment

Decide on a worthwhile topic for testing, and devise a short test. Plan how you are going to manage the test in the classroom and how you will evaluate the results. Conduct the test and evaluate the results.

Did your test provide useful information?

How will you use it?

Can you use the data to inform your teaching?

Can you set targets for the group/individuals?

5   Evaluating different methods of gathering assessment evidence

Draw up a three-column table, with some chosen techniques for gathering assessment evidence listed on the left, and two adjacent columns for the advantages and disadvantages of each. Fill in the table bearing in mind:

Why gather evidence in this way?

For whom is this assessment being done?

What can be most appropriately monitored in this way?

How often might this technique be used?

In what situations can this technique be used?

How can the results be interpreted?

Are there any unforeseen effects of such assessment?

Are the techniques valid and free from cultural bias?

Having made your own decisions about the 'pros' and 'cons' of different techniques for gathering assessment evidence, you should now be in a position to choose which techniques you will use for various purposes, and in which contexts. This should help you to devise a flexible and powerful set of techniques to assess processes and products within your classroom.

7 Opening up the secret garden of assessment

Readers who have come this far in our exploration of assessment for learning should now be in no doubt about two things. First, that assessment is probably the most profound influence on what gets learned, when learning occurs and who does the learning. Second that assessment *FOR* learning is probably the most neglected topic in the whole of the educational world, whether this is educational policy making, educational research or educational practice itself. Why this should be so is not our primary concern here. Suffice it to say that it has a great deal to do with the extraordinarily important role that educational assessment has played over the last 100 years or so as a mechanism for testifying competence and allocating individual life chances. In our legitimate and pressing concern to devise fair and manageable instruments for this purpose, we have arguably lost track of the most important assessment issue of all: namely how it can help or hinder pupils' learning. The rapid expansion of both traditional forms of educational provision at the present time, particularly at the post-16 stage, and the development of radically new opportunities for learning through technological developments, has begun to shift the focus of debate back onto learning itself and how we can create individuals able and keen to profit from these new opportunities. As a result, there has been a significant growth of interest in recent years in *assessment for learning*.

This book is one manifestation of that interest. In it we have argued the pressing need for the educational community as a whole to recognise the crucial part played by assessment within each individual's learning career, and hence the need for teachers to have the same level of insight and skill in managing their use of it in the classroom as they have in relation to any other aspect of professional practice.

Indeed, we would put the point even more strongly. We have suggested that getting classroom assessment right is even more important than pedagogical issues or curriculum content for it is assessment that influences fundamentally a pupil's attitude to learning. It is an overworked cliché to say that you can take a horse to water but you cannot make it drink, but every teacher knows it is true. The difference between teaching a motivated child and an unmotivated child is the world. A child who is curious, confident and engaged is a delight to teach. A child who is apathetic and afraid to try or one who protects their self-esteem through hostility to the learning process is a problem all too familiar to most teachers.

In the government's headlong pursuit of higher educational standards in recent years, virtually all the attention has been given to the quality of schools, their management and the way in which individual teachers 'deliver' the curriculum. The pupil is seen as a passive 'letterbox' which will receive the 'letters' delivered by the postman provided they are the right size and shape to fit it. This is a woefully misconceived view of the educational process. Learning is an interactive relationship. It is something that happens when the engagement between teacher and taught results in a positive and meaningful communication for the pupil. Pupils not only construct their own understanding based on their existing insights, knowledge and skills; they will persevere or give up, take risks or exercise caution, remember or forget, depending on their *feelings*. Whether they like the teacher, the subject, the classroom group; whether they have problems at home or with their peers at school – these are all factors that impact on the success of the learning encounter. So much is well known and well recognised by teachers on a day-to-day basis. Much less well known, sadly, is the particular part played by assessment in creating such positive or negative feelings and in supporting or hindering pupils in their learning journeys.

This book has been concerned with illuminating some of these profoundly important aspects of the relationship between assessment and learning. In Chapter 1 we explored some of the limitations of the current 'standards' agenda: how it focuses too narrowly on what can be measured rather than on what is important; how, despite the overall increase in levels of performance, it is leading to a widening gulf between both successful and unsuccessful schools and successful and unsuccessful pupils. We discussed the need for a change of focus in the light of the new challenges facing education if it is to prepare pupils for life and work in the twenty-first century, and we deplored how little attention has been given in the educational community as a whole to defining what is good learning rather than what is good teaching.

In Chapter 2 we broadened and deepened this general discussion in terms of what psychology can tell us about the impact of assessment on pupils' learning orientations. From this evidence it is clear that self-esteem, so central to success both in school and in life more generally, according to recent research, is all too often eroded by the experience of negative evaluations. According to the assessment climate that has been created, students will tend to develop either a 'trading for grades' mentality or a real desire to master the topic in hand for their own satisfaction. Those who repeatedly fail may well develop 'learned help-lessness' – an unwillingness to try in order that they can attribute any subsequent failure to lack of effort rather than lack of ability.

In English classrooms, notions of 'ability', 'intelligence', being 'bright' or not are much more pervasive than in many other countries such as France or Japan where differences in pupils' performance are much more likely to be attributed to effort. One consequence of this is that pupils tend to form self-assessments quite early in their school lives as to whether they are 'clever' or not (Pollard, *et al.*, 2000), judgements which profoundly affect the way in which they engage in learning in the future. (The way in which pupils' identities as learners develop has been documented in a series of detailed longitudinal studies of individual pupils by Andrew Pollard and Ann Filer, 1999.) The recent increase in the prominence of assessment that 'categorises' pupils by levels and grades and predicts their subsequent performance on this basis appears to be powerfully reinforcing the effects of such early stereotyping. Hence the policy would seem to be having quite the opposite effect from the one intended in that it is tending to dampen the aspirations of a significant number of pupils.

Also in Chapter 2, we explored the positive psychological benefits that can accrue from assessment that is designed to *support* learning. There is now a considerable body of evidence to support the view that when students are trained in the skills of reflection, self-assessment and personal target-setting; when they experience success rather than failure and are clear what they need to do to improve as a result of the right kind of feedback, there is likely to be a significant impact on learning. In their survey of the research literature relating to assessment for learning which they conducted for ARG and to which we have referred throughout this book, Paul Black and Dylan Wiliam (1998a) identify five simple key factors:

- the provision of effective feedback to pupils
- the active involvement of pupils in their own learning
- adjusting teaching to take account of the results of assessment
- a recognition of the profound influence assessment has on the motivation and self-esteem of pupils and hence on their learning
- the need for pupils to be able to assess themselves and understand how to improve.

They go on to argue that for assessment to support learning, it must be conceived as a core part of the teaching and learning process. Pupils need to be clear what it is they are supposed to be learning and why, and to have a clear picture of the standards they are aiming for. Pupils themselves, as well as teachers, need to be able and willing to use assessment data to determine next steps. Perhaps most important of all is confidence on the part of both teacher and pupil that *every* student can improve. As one French secondary school headteacher has put it, 'I show the children the plants in the playground and I point out that even if I water them all in the same way, some will flower quicker than others, but all of them will flower. And all children will succeed even if some of them need more time' (*Le Monde de L'Education*, June 1995: 50).

So even in the world of education, where there are often conflicting messages about 'what works', the research evidence concerning how assessment should be designed to support learning provides an unusually powerful and unambiguous message. Empower students with their own assessment skills, provide them with the right kinds of guidance and have confidence in their success.

Sadly, however, we seem to be very far from acting upon this message as yet. As we saw in Chapters 3 and 4, the evidence from the LEARN project suggests that pupils at all stages of the education system may have a good surface understanding of the individual task in which they are engaged, but typically have very little understanding of the overall purpose of the task as part of a larger whole. Pupils, especially lower attainers, are dependent on teachers who control and direct class activity. Feedback tends to focus on a rather limited range of criteria and pupils often do not know the significance of a particular grade or mark. Moreover, the study found very little evidence of genuine self-assessment. These findings support those of Paul Black and Dylan Wiliam's literature review which suggested that teachers do not know enough about pupils' individual learning needs, tend to assess the quantity and presentation of work rather than the quality of learning it represents and give greater attention to marking and grading than to providing advice for improvement. These factors, combined with a tendency to emphasise comparison between pupils, have the effect of demoralising less successful learners. Black and Wiliam also found that teachers' feedback to pupils often serves social and managerial purposes rather than being aimed at helping them to learn more effectively.

The story that we have told in this book is both an optimistic and a pessimistic one. On the positive side, we now know very clearly how important assessment is within the learning process and this importance is beginning to be recognised at all levels of the education system. On the negative side is the evidence that we have a long way to go as an educational community in terms of putting the principles identified in this book into practice. There is no lack of goodwill. Teachers up and down the country are excited by the powerful possibilities of effective formative assessment – assessment for learning. At the same time, however, the relentless imperative of league tables and exam results appears to require both teachers' and pupils' energies to be invested in a very different direction.

Can this tension be resolved? This is the question that ARG addresses in its 1999 pamphlet *Assessment for Learning: Beyond the Black Box*. In it, ARG considers the gap that currently exists between the evidence of what needs to be done and the evidence of what is currently characteristic of classroom assessment practice and makes recommendations for what could be done by government to resolve the issue. Suggestions include training teachers in formative assessment techniques during both initial training and continuing professional development, providing funds to support schools in the development of exemplar materials and perhaps most important of all, making assessment for learning a central focus of the policy programme for raising standards. All of these are important and valuable suggestions. But in this book we have taken a rather different approach. We have painted a picture of the reality of assessment as experienced by school pupils of different ages and kinds ranging from A level and GNVQ at one extreme to the end of key stage 1 at the other. We have shown in Chapter 5 how often the time and effort invested in marking work is not understood by pupils in a way that helps them to make improvements; we have used pupils' own voices to depict the reality of success and failure as they experience it; the apparent arbitrariness for them of so much of the learning game; the unforeseen effects of current policy that can turn an eager infant into an anxious junior almost overnight. If, by so doing, we have established the need for action, this in itself is worthwhile.

Hopefully, though, we have done more than this in pointing the way to action; in suggesting activities that teachers, individually and in groups, can undertake now in order to improve things in their own particular school. We do not have to wait for government to see the light and lessen the choking constraints of the standards agenda in its current form. We do not have to wait for more research and more exemplar material to be available, desirable as these would be. We do not even need to wait for teachers to receive more training in the skills of using assessment to support learning, though this will clearly need to be made available. The tasks and activities throughout this book, along with the suggestions for action in Chapter 6, provide the basis for all schools to discover what's in it for them in promoting assessment for learning.

This is not a transition that will be achieved overnight but neither is it likely to be a short-lived educational fashion, a bandwagon like those before it that will come and go leaving little trace. Rather a shift in the centre of gravity from assessment that merely measures and certifies towards assessment as an integral and planned element of the learning process is the tip of an iceberg of change that during the twenty-first century will put the learner, rather than the teacher or the curriculum, or even the external examination, increasingly at the heart of educational debates. The 'secret garden' of assessment has kept learners in thrall for long enough.

If we ask what's in it for schools, the answer is a simple one: our vision is the prospect of *all* pupils being enthusiastic and effective learners. This is surely an outcome worth fighting for.

References and further reading

Abbot, J. (1999) 'Battery hens or free range chickens: what kind of education for what kind of world?', *Journal of the 21st Century Learning Initiative*, Jan.: 1–12.

ACAC (1997) *Geography KS3 Optional Tasks and Tests*, Cardiff: ACAC.

Airasian, P. (1996) *Assessment in the Classroom*, New York: McGraw-Hill.

Alberge, D. (1999) 'Author brings stifling school system to book', *The Times*, 15 July 1999: 16.

Apple, M. W. (1989) 'How equality has been redefined in the conservative restoration', in W. Secada (ed.) *Equity and Education*, New York: Falmer.

Arnot, M., Gray, J., James, M., Rudduck, J. and Duveen, G. (1996) *Gender and Educational Performance: A Review of Recent Research*, London: Ofsted.

Assessment Reform Group (ARG) (1999) *Assessment for Learning: Beyond the Black Box*, Cambridge: ARG.

Ausubel, D. P. (1960) 'The use of advanced organisers in the learning and retention of meaningful verbal material', *Journal of Educational Psychology* 51: 267–72.

Black, P. (1998) *Testing: Friend or Foe? Theory and Practice of Assessment and Testing*, London: Falmer.

Black, P. and Wiliam, D. (1998a) *Inside the Black Box*, London: Kings College.

Black, P. and Wiliam, D. (1998b) 'Assessment and classroom learning', *Assessment in Education* 5.1: 7–74.

Blunkett, D. (2000) '*New drive on secondary school standards*', speech to the North of England Education Conference.
http://www.dfes.gov.uk/pns/DisplayPN.cgi?pn_id=2000_0002

Boud, D. (1995) *Enhancing Learning through Self Assessment*, London: Kogan Page.

Broadfoot, P. (1996) 'The myth of measurement' in P. Woods (ed.) *Contemporary Issues in Teaching and Learning*, London: Routledge.

Broadfoot, P. and Pollard, A. (2000) 'The changing discourse of assessment policy: the case of English primary education', in A. Filer, *Assessment: Social Practice and Social Product*, London: RoutledgeFalmer.

Butt, G., Lambert, D. and Telfer S. (1995) *Assessment Works: Approaches to Assessment in Geography at Key Stages 1, 2 and 3*, Sheffield: Geographical Association.

Centre for Assessment Studies, University of Bristol (1992) *A Whole School Assessment Policy, Key Stage 2 and Beyond*, Windsor: NFER-NELSON.

Clarke, S. (1998) *Targeting Assessment in the Primary School*, London: Hodder & Stoughton.

Claxton, G. (1998) *Mastering Uncertainty: The New Science of Lifelong Learning*, University of Bristol Mimeo.

Curtis, R., Weeden, P. and Winter, J. (2000) 'Intuition and assessment in three subject areas', in G. Claxton and T. Atkinson (eds) *The Intuitive Practitioner*, Milton Keynes: Open University Press.

Daugherty, R. (1995) *National Curriculum Assessment: A Review of Policy 1987–1994*, London: Falmer.

DES/WO (1988) *National Curriculum Task Group on Assessment and Testing: A Report*, London: DES/WO.

DfEE (1997) *From Targets to Action*, London: DfEE.

Fullan, M. (1991) *The New Meaning of Educational Change*, London: Cassell.

Gillborn, D. and Gipps, C. (1996) *Recent research on the Achievements of Ethnic Minority Pupils*, London: OFSTED.

Gipps, C. and Murphy, P. (1994) *A Fair Test? Assessment, Achievement and Equity*, Buckingham: Open University Press.

GOAL (2001) *On-line Assessment System*, www.goalplc.co.uk

Handy, C. (1994) *The Empty Raincoat: Making Sense of the Future*, London: Hutchinson.

Harris, D. and Bell, C. (1986) *Evaluating and Assessing for Learning*, London: Kogan Page.

James, D. (2000) 'Making the graduate: perspectives on student experience of assessment in higher education', in A. Filer (ed.) *Assessment: Social Practice and Social Product*, London: RoutledgeFalmer.

James, M. (1998) *Using Assessment for School Improvement*, Oxford: Heinemann.

Jones, R. L. and Bray, E. (1986) *Assessment: From Principles to Action*, London: Macmillan.

Kluger, A. N. and DeNisi, A. (1996) 'The effects of feedback interventions on performance: a historical view, a meta-analysis, and a preliminary feedback intervention theory', *Psychological Bulletin*, 119.2: 254–84.

Lambert, D. and Lines, D. (2000) *Understanding Assessment: Purposes, Perceptions, Practices*, London: RoutledgeFalmer.

Le Monde de L'Education June 1995, Paris.

Madaus, G. (1988) 'The influence of testing on the curriculum', in L. Tanner (ed.), *Critical Issues in Curriculum, 87th Yearbook of NSSE Part 1*, Chicago: University of Chicago Press.

Murphy, P. (1995) 'Assessment-gender implications', in D. Farrelly (ed.), *Examinations in the Context of Change*, Dublin: University College Dublin.

Neesom, A. (2000) *Teacher's Perception of Formative Assessment*, London: QCA.

OFSTED (1998) *Secondary Education 1993–97: A Review of Secondary Schools in England*, London: HMSO.

OFSTED (1999) *Primary Education 1994–98: A Review of Primary Schools in England*, London: HMSO.

Pollard, A. and Filer, A. (1999) *The Social World of Pupil Career*, London: Cassell.

Pollard, A. and Triggs, P. (1997) *Reflective Teaching in Secondary Education*, London: Cassell.

Pollard, A. and Triggs, P. with Broadfoot, P., McNess, E. and Osborn, M. (2000) *What Pupils Say: Changing Policy and Practice in Primary Education*, London: Continuum.

QCA (2001a) *Standards at Key Stage 2: English, Mathematics and Science*, London: QCA.

QCA (2001b) *Standards at Key Stage 3: English*, London: QCA.

QCA (2001c) *Five Yearly Review of Standards Report*.
http://www.qca.org/nq/mar/summary.asp

QCA (2002) http://www.qca.org.uk/nq/framework/

Reineke, R. A. (1998) *Challenging the Mind, Touching the Heart: Best Assessment Practices*, Thousand Oaks, CA: Corwin Oaks.

Rogers, C. (1994) 'A common basis for success', in P. Kutnick and C. Rogers, *Groups in Schools*, London: Cassell.

Ross, M. (ed.) (1986) *Assessment in Arts Education*, Oxford: Pergamon Press.

Rudduck, J., Chaplain, R. and Wallace, G. (1996) *School Improvement: What Can Pupils Tell Us?*, London: David Fulton.

Sadler, D. R. (1989) 'Formative assessment and the design of instructional systems', *Instructional Science* 18: 119–44.

Satterly, D. (1989) *Assessment in schools*, 2nd edn, Oxford: Basil Blackwell.

SCAA (School Curriculum and Assessment Authority) (1995) *Consistency in Teacher Assessment: Guidance for Schools*, London: SCAA.

Sutton, R. (1991) *Assessment: A Framework for Teachers*, London: Routledge.

Steinberg, R. (1996) *Beyond the Classroom: Why School Reform has Failed and What Parents Need to Do*, New York: Touchstone.

Sternberg, R. J. (1966) 'Myths, countermyths and truths about intelligence', *Educational Researcher* 25.2: 85–98.

Stobart, G. and Gipps, C. (1997) *Assessment: A Teacher's Guide to the Issues*, 3rd edn, London: Hodder & Stoughton.

Summerskill, B. (2000) 'All the advantages? They'll fail without self-esteem', *Observer* 24 Sept. 2000: 4.

Sylva, K. (1994) 'School influences on children's development', *Journal of Child Psychology and Psychiatry*, 35.1: 135–70.

Sylvester, R. (1995) *A Celebration of Neurons*, New York: ASCD.

Times Educational Supplement (2001) 'Target Practice', TES extra on Birmingham (2 Mar. 2001), p. 3.

Tunstall, P. and Gipps, C. (1995) 'Teacher feedback to young children in formative assessment: a typology', paper given to the International Association of Educational Assessment (IAEA), Montreal, June.

Weeden, P. and Winter, J. (1999) *The LEARN Project: Report for QCA*, London: QCA.

Wiliam, D. (1996) 'Standard-setting methods for multiple levels of competence', in B. Boyle and T. Christie (eds) *Issues in Setting Standards*, London: Falmer.

Wiliam, D. (2000) 'Recent developments in educational assessment in England: the integration of formative and summative functions of assessment', ARG conference, Bristol. Paper first presented at the first meeting of the Scientific Advisory Board for the Swedish National Mathematics and Science Tests (SweMas) held at the University of Umeå, May 2000.

Wiliam, D. and Black, P. (1996) 'Meanings and consequences: a basis for distinguishing formative and summative functions of assessment?', *British Educational Research Journal*, 22.5: 537–48.

Wintle, M. and Harrison, M. (1999) *Co-ordinating Assessment Practice Across the Primary School*, Subject Leader's Handbook series, London: Falmer.

Wragg, T. (1997) *Assessment and Learning*, London: Routledge.

Index

Assessment is not used as a main heading since it is the main subject of the text.

A level 1, 2, 3, 32–3, 34, 49
ability 56
accountability 145
achievement: raising 123; recording 101, 144–6
action planning 140
action points 130–2, 143–4, 146
activities 17, 39, 69–71, 93–4, 119–21, 147–9; for pupils 84, 86
advanced organisers 55, 76, 107
affective factors 49
Airasian, Peter 77
alienation 62
Almond, David 7–8
anxiety 15
ARG (Assessment Reform Group) 24, 30, 38, 154
assessed work, using examples of 87
assessment evidence *see* data/ analysis/collection
assessment goals 9–11
assessment for learning *see* formative assessment
assessment of learning *see* summative assessment
Assessment Reform Group (ARG) 24, 30, 38, 154
assumptions 11–12

Best Practice Research Studentships (DfES) 127
Birmingham LEA 62
Black, Paul 18, 19, 24, 25, 29, 35, 41, 53, 72, 104, 110, 153, 154
Boud, David 74, 118
boys' performance 59–61, 64–8

case studies 25–7
certification 31
change management 126–9
Clarke, Shirley 57, 85
Claxton, Guy 9
classification of assessment 19–20
closed-response tests 142–3
cognitive testing 141
comments 103–4, 110, 125, 129, 145–6
competition 44
computer-based testing 105, 143
conferencing 140
conservatism 127
content 64
context 68
continuity 144–5
creativity, stifling of 6–8
criteria for assessment: pupils' understanding of 46–7, 83–4; sharing with pupils 85–6
criterion-referenced tests 141
cues 109

current practice 125–6; improvement in 40–71

data /analysis/collection 56, 132–44; existing data, use of 36, 134
debates 137
diagnostic assessment 19
differential performance 61, 62, 68
differentiation 52
disaffection 62
discussion 88, 137
Dweck, Carol 53

education, assumptions about 11–12
educational outcomes, equity in 59–61
effective learning 41
emotion, role in learning 14–16, 79
empowerment 6–9, 16, 36
entry patterns 65
equity 58–68; in educational outcomes 59–61, 68; meaning of 58–9
ethnicity 59–64, 68
evaluative assessment 19, 20
evidence *see* data/analysis/collection
examination results 3
examinations 143
expectations 64

failure 16
fairness 58–68
feedback 95–121; as aid to improving learning 104–7, 109–10; effectiveness of 118–19; guidelines for 118; issues associated with 110–13; more effective use of 113–18; principles of 96–101; pupils' responses to 101–4, 108–9, 112–13; and record keeping 113; tests 114–15; timing of 100, 115; types of 101–2; verbal 116

Filer, Ann 152
form 64
formative assessment 12, 13–14, 23; benefits of 28; challenges for teachers 28–9; definition 19, 20; promise, reality and challenges of 24–7; raising standards through 36–8
From Targets to Action (DfEE) 56
funding 127

GCSE 1, 3, 32, 34, 35, 45–6, 48, 49, 59, 85
gender 51, 59, 61
Gillborn, David 59–61
Gipps, Caroline 59–61, 68
girls' performance 59–61, 64–8
GNVQ 2, 32–3, 47, 49
goal-orientation 27, 48–9
good practice 40
Goodhart's Law 19
grades 31, 125, 152; and learning objectives 114; and pupil performance 110–11; pupils' understanding of 102–3; v. comments 129

HEI (Higher Education Institutions) 38, 128
'high stakes' testing 33–4, 35
higher attainers 46, 48
Higher Education Institutions (HEI) 38, 128

improvement in current practice 40–71; in learning 104–7; in performance 64–5; in standards 18–19
individuals, knowledge of 37
information *see* data
information systems 128
interviews 45, 83, 88

James, Mary 65, 87, 125
journals 88
judgements 135–6

key areas for development 124
Key Stage 1 (KS1): classroom-based
tasks 21; tests 1, 30; transition to
KS3 21–2, 134
Key Stage 2 (KS2) tests 1, 30, 49, 73
Key Stage 3 (KS3) 21
knowledge 63; of individuals 37
KS *see* Key Stages

labelling 55, 128
Lambert, David 105
language 66
LEARN project 4, 5, 15, 44–5, 50,
80, 139, 153
learned helplessness 52, 55, 108, 152
learner motivation styles 55–6
learners, pupils as 2
learning improvement in 104–7, 123,
130; nature of 8; new types of 9;
promotion of 122; role of emotion
in 14–16, *see also* effective learning;
mastery learning
learning briefing sheets 76, 78
learning function 44
learning goals *see* learning objectives
learning intentions 86, 130, 132
learning objectives 27, 86, 97, 114
learning outcomes 64, 86, 97–8, 100
learning, promotion of 2, 4–5;
through assessment 12–13, 41;
through self-assessment 75–6
learning strategies 77; and self-
assessment 84–5
learning styles 66
Level Descriptions (National
Curriculum) 106, 112, 114
level of response mark scheme 106
Lines, David 105
listening 137
long-termism 16
low achievers 26–7, 44, 49, 52–8, 83,
93, 116–17
lower attainers 45

McNamara Fallacy 10
Madaus, George 34

manageability 20–3
managerial function 44
mark schemes 104–7
marking 64, 95–121; as assessment
data 139; comments 129;
effectiveness of 118–19; grades
129; principles of 96–101;
prioritising 98, 100; similarity of
116; use of to improve learning
104–7
marks 31, 145–6
mastery learning 25, 53, 54,
108
mastery tests 141
measurement of standards
18–19
meta-cognitive skills 76
misconceptions 98, 138
mode of assessment 65–8
motivation 25; effect of feedback
on 111–12; factors affecting
47–8; learner styles 55–6; links
with teaching and self-assessment
77–9; and low achievers 52–8
Murphy, Patricia 66

National Curriculum 1, 12, 20, 21,
35, 80, 107, 114, 130
National Foundation for Educational
Research (NFER) 125
National Qualifications Framework
(NQF) 32–3
negative effects on learning 42–4,
152
NFER (National Foundation for
Educational Research) 125
norm-referenced tests 141
norm-referencing 125

O-level results 3
objectivity 63, 64, 65, 105
observation 135–7
OFSTED reports 1, 13, 18, 40, 52,
59, 62, 63, 95, 125
open-response tests 142–3
oral assessment 137

PACE (Primary, Assessment, Curriculum and Expectations) project 8, 15
PANDAs (Performance and Assessment Reports) 128
parents 146
partnerships 75
peer assessment 85, 89–90
Performance and Assessment Reports (PANDAs) 128
performance goals 27
performance, improvement in 64
performance indicators 19
performance measurement 35, 62
'performance'-oriented pupils 54–5
personal reflection 144
planning 132, 133; and improvement 130; schools policies 126, 128; and self-assessment 84, 85–6
point-credit mark scheme 104–6
polarisation 52
Pollard, Andrew 8, 152
portfolios 88–9, 125, 145
presentations 137
Primary, Assessment, Curriculum and Expectations (PACE) project 8, 15
primary schools 1
prioritising marking 98, 100
progress review 140
progression 144–5
promotion of learning 122
public examinations 143
published tests 142
pupil culture 52
pupils as learners 2; perspective of 80–1; reactions to written comments 103–4; responses to feedback 101–4, 108–9, 112–13; training 114
purposes of assessment 19–20, 23, 36, 87, 117–18

qualifications 32–3
Qualifications and Curriculum Authority (QCA) 1, 4, 14, 45
questioning 137

rationalising marking 98, 100
record-keeping 89; action point 146; forms of 101, 145–6; links with feedback 113; purposes of 144–5; and self-assessment 84, *see also* reports on pupils
Record of Achievement (RoA) 124
reflection 144, 152
reflective assessment 26–7
reliability 20–3, 105
reports on pupils 31, 144–6, 145–6, 146
response 66
review processes 74, 86–7, 90, 140
RoA (Record of Achievement) 124
Rogers, Colin 53, 54
roles 74–5, 81–2, 132–3

school policies 123–30; as agents of change 126–7, 128–9; content 125, 128; format 125, 128; implementation 125, 128; planning 126, 128; and raising standards 130; review 126, 128; self-assessment 126, 129; target-setting 126, 129
schools assumptions about 11–12; current situation 79–84; issues for consideration 41; making a difference 56
self-assessment 72–94; ability of pupils to undertake 83; definition 73–4; examples 80; importance in learning process 75; and learning 72–94, 140; and learning strategies 84–5; links with teaching and motivation 77–9; as new way of thinking 74; Portugal case study 25–6; problems of implementation 91–2; pupils' perspective 80; and school policies 126, 129
self-esteem 15, 16, 25, 152
self-evaluation *see* self-assessment
self-perception 31
self-reliance 9

SEN (Special Educational Needs) 133
short-termism 16
SMART 37–8, 108
social class 59–61, 68
social constructs, standards as 31–2
social context 64
Special Educational Needs (SEN)
  133
standards limitations of 18–19; in
  qualifications 32; raising 18–39,
  130; rising 1–2, 13, 31–2; as social
  constructs 31–2
Stobart, Gordon 68
subject-based testing 141
success in school work 51, 56
summative assessment 13–14, 16, 23;
  definition 19, 20, 29; promise,
  reality and challenges of 29–30,
  32–3; and promotion of learning
  30–1; and records 145
support for learning 152

target-setting 37, 50–1, 56–8, 117,
  126, 129
Task Group on Assessment and
  Testing (1988) (TGAT) 12–14, 20,
  21, 122
task-setting 138
teacher assessment 23
teacher dependence 4, 45, 81, 84
teacher expectations 28
teacher tests 142

teachers
teachers:beliefs v. actions 42; role of
  132–3
teaching enhancement through
  assessment 123, 130; informing
  through recording information
  144; links with self-assessment and
  motivation 77–9
testing/tests 33–4, 114–15, 141–3
TGAT (Task Group on Assessment
  and Testing) (1988) 12–14, 20, 21,
  122
time issues 85, 90
timing of feedback 115
training pupils 114

under-achievement *see* low achievers
under performance 59

validity 20–3; everyday tasks 138;
  and performance 64; and point-
  credit mark schemes 105;
  summative assessment 30
verbal feedback 116

Wiliam, Dylan 18, 19, 20, 24, 25, 29,
  31–2, 35, 41, 72, 104, 110, 153,
  154
written comments, pupils' reactions
  to 103–4

Youth Cohort Study 60